The Smart Classroom Management Way

10 Years of Writing From the Top Classroom Management Blog in the World

Michael Linsin

JME Publishing
San Diego, California
smartclassroommanagement.com

Edited by Christine Haack

ISBN: 9781795512848

Contents

Introduction

I N 2009, I STARTED a blog called Smart Classroom Management (SCM) because I felt I had to. Literally. I'd spent the previous 18 years focused on little more than testing and perfecting the most effective classroom management strategies I could find or invent myself and distilling them into a single, unified approach. I was at the point in my journey where I just *knew* that any teacher could apply the same simple methods I was using and replicate my success.

I was working at an especially challenging school at the time. My colleagues were stressed out, exhausted, and up to their eyeballs with misbehavior. My experience, however, couldn't have been more different. My students were happy. They were hardworking. They were mature and well behaved. And I was enjoying every minute of it. I couldn't wait to get to school each day and was easily the first teacher to leave campus in the afternoon. I felt as if I'd discovered the secret to perfect health or easy money, and I just had to get the word out. I had to share what I knew with as many teachers as possible or I wouldn't be able to live with myself. So on May 25th, 2009 I posted my first article to smartclassroommanagement.com.

In the years since, I've written more than 500 articles, three e-guides, and five books, including the precursor to this one called *The Classroom Management Secret* (2013). The blog has grown to more than 125,000 subscribers, millions of readers, and thousands of email success stories. But way back in 2009, as I crafted that first article, I had in mind that one day I would take the very best strategies—those that resonated most with readers and had the greatest effect on student behavior—and assemble them into a single volume.

When I first started putting this book together more than a year ago, it became important to me that it wasn't simply a random mix of popular articles (some of which have been shared via social media more than 100,000 times), but rather a comprehensive work that included every principle, theme, and methodology of the SCM approach. With the help of a few trusted associates, I think we've done just that.

The book is laid out across six major areas of classroom management and includes the most pressing issues, problems, and concerns shared by all teachers. The underlying SCM themes of accountability, maturity, independence, personal responsibility, and intrinsic motivation are all there and weave their way throughout the entirety of the book. Together, they form a simple, unique, and sometimes contrarian approach to classroom management that *anyone* can do.

It's important to note that as you work your way through the book, or visit particular articles or sections most interesting to you, you'll notice references to the use of a classroom management plan. Rest assured, you'll find the exact elementary and high school plans I recommend, as well as advice for middle school teachers, on the SCM website.

The previous ten years of running SCM have been a labor of love, and I'm thrilled to share what I believe to be the easiest, most effective way to manage today's students and inspire them to their highest potential. Whether you're new to SCM or one of our loyal readers, *The Smart Classroom Management Way* will help you unlock your love and passion for teaching and give you the tools you need to be the best, happiest, and most popular teacher at your school.

PART ONE:
First Things

6 Things You Must Do on the First Day of School

YOU HAVE ONE OPPORTUNITY to start your school year on the right classroom management foot, one shot to propel your first day of school into the best learning experience your students have ever had. You can't afford to leave it to chance. You can't afford to be unprepared, uninspired, or unfocused. You can't afford to be anything other than on top of your game. For a lasting first impression will set the tone for the rest of the school year.

It will set the tone for behavior, work habits, respect, responsibility, camaraderie, and so much more. Thus, your first day of school should reflect your vision of a dream class. It should reflect who you are, what you expect, and what it means to be a member of your special classroom. It should stir in your students the desire to become more or better or somehow different than when they walked through your door.

What follows are six things that, when infused with your passion and conviction, and sprinkled with a dose of your wonderful imperfection, will make your first day of school one your students won't soon forget.

1. Make a connection.

Building rapport begins the moment your students lay eyes on you. Greet them with a smile and let them know in no uncertain terms that you're glad they're a member of your class and now part of a unique community. Your initial friendliness and open, welcoming heart will put them at ease and spark an immediate desire to please you, follow your lead, and pay forward your kindness throughout the classroom.

2. Set a tone of excellence.

After just a few introductory remarks, send the message that you expect excellence in everything they do by showing your students how you expect them to enter the classroom in the morning. Make it highly detailed, demonstrating every precious step. This first routine, when taught with depth and precision, and then practiced successfully, paves the way for all other routines to be learned quickly and thereafter performed with excellence.

3. Have some fun.

Whether it's a getting to know you game, a rollicking story of your youth, or just your everyday humor, be sure your students see, and experience, that being in your classroom also means having fun. It's key to not only their motivation and attentiveness and instilling a love for learning, but it also affords you the leverage and influential presence to ask for and expect hard work, respect, and kind behavior from your students.

4. Make a promise.

By now your students will be buzzing with the understanding that yours is no ordinary classroom. The startling expectations, the joyful learning, and the quiet thrill in their heart is evidence enough that it's going to be a remarkable year. They are now primed to hear from you a most important promise, a promise that will largely determine your and their success. You're going to promise them that you will protect their special community, that you will protect their right to learn and enjoy school.

5. Fulfill your promise.
When students understand its true purpose—that is, a safeguard against interruptions, disrespect, name-calling, etc.—your classroom management plan takes on a whole new meaning. Rather than being viewed as a negative, it will be seen for what it is: a means to preserve their love of school. Teach your plan, not as a hard-edged disciplinarian, but as one who cares enough about their education to defend it to the hilt. Although you'll spend parts of the rest of the week modeling and practicing your plan, a detailed overview on the first day is a must.

6. Dive headlong into academics.
Establish from the get-go that your classroom is in the business of learning by diving into a challenging academic lesson (or two or three) on the first day of school. Be sure, however, that it's spot-on—high interest, participatory, leaving no doubt as to what you want your students *to know* and *to do*. Their success understanding and then performing your first academic objective is crucial to their confidence going forward, setting the stage for limitless improvement.

Beautiful Imperfection

Although the six items above won't be all you'll do on the first day of school, they are the most important. It's a mistake, though, to assume that because they're important, you have to be perfect. You don't—far from it. Have your content, your objectives, and the overall tone of the day pictured clearly in your mind, but allow yourself room to mess up, to stumble over your words (or the trash bin you forgot was behind your desk), and to pause and consider what to say next.

In this way, your natural, influence-building charisma will shine through. So let go of any and all pressure to be perfect—self-imposed or otherwise. Let go of the what-ifs and the negative trains of thought. Let go of the pressure to perform. Take a long, slow, deep breath and exhale it all out into the ether, saying good-bye forever. Just be you and your students will love you for it.

How a First-Day-of-School Lesson Can Improve Classroom Management for the Rest of the Year

T HERE EXISTS A STRATEGY that, if taught on the first day of school, can have a profound effect on the rest of the year. It takes little if any preparation time. It's simple in its directness and also fun and participatory. But it will shake your students down to the soles of their feet. It will send the message that yours is no ordinary classroom, that expectations have taken a startling leap skyward . . . that they're not in Kansas anymore.

You see, one of the best things you can do on the first day of school is set the bar of what is normal far above what your students are used to. Far above what your colleagues are doing. Far above what most teachers mean when they use the term "high expectations."

The good news is that you can make this leap in a single lesson. You can rewire your students' internal understanding of excellence in one short but electric block of time. It's a lesson they'll readily accept without so much as an eye roll because they'll assume that in your class, your grade level, or your subject area, *it's just the way things are.*

Furthermore, on the first day of school your students will be more open to change than at any other time during the year. They're primed and ready to start fresh, to turn over a new leaf, to put the mistakes and failures of the past behind them.

How It Works

The way the strategy works is that you're going to teach your students a common, everyday routine—like how to enter the classroom in the morning—in a way that is highly, minutely, even obsessively, detailed. You're going to teach it in a way that redefines what it means to follow directions and perform at a high level, while at the same time ensuring that every student is successful.

Done right, this new definition of excellence will transfer to every area of classroom management, from behavior to motivation to politeness. It will establish a standard that will continue for as long as you maintain it. Teaching this bar-raising strategy entails creating a memory map for your students to follow *every single morning.*

Here's how:

You Model

Borrow a student's backpack and, while pretending to be an actual member of your class, perform the morning routine precisely how you want your students to do it. Show purpose, expediency, and concentration as you model your way through the steps you want them to take upon entering your classroom.

This may include hanging up backpacks and jackets, checking mailboxes, organizing personal materials, and displaying or turning in homework. It may include greeting tablemates or reviewing the daily schedule. It's smart to *add* details rather than making it too simple.

Challenge is good and will increase concentration, improve memory, and keep your students focused and purpose-driven from the moment they walk through the door. Extend the routine to the point where they're either working independently or sitting quietly, facing you, and ready to begin the first lesson.

A specific, well-oiled routine will eliminate morning apathy, irritability, sleepiness, silliness, and the like, ensuring a peaceful rather than stressful start to each day. It also saves time and allows you to be a *teacher* rather than a micromanager.

Student Models

After modeling twice, and asking your students if they have any clarifying questions, choose a single student to model. Ask them to mimic your actions and movements, and even your focused expressions, in minute detail.

When they finish, calmly praise them for what they did well. Remember, praise is both effective and worthy when students are learning something for the first time. It provides feedback that further illuminates the path you want them to follow. Having one student model causes the rest to visualize themselves doing it right along with them. It also proves that it can be done, and done well.

If, however, even one step strays from your initial instruction, then point it out, reteach it, and have the student do it again. It is the smallest details that make the biggest difference. Done correctly, you should feel as if you're going overboard in your instruction.

More Model

Now call on a few more students to model, one at a time, for the class. Follow them as they go through the steps and movements, nodding along the way. Use papers, books, umbrellas, laptops, and sweaters as props. Make it as close to the real thing as you can. Again, if corners are cut, ask them to start over again from the beginning. Have the mindset that you're only going to teach this particular routine one time. So teach the heck out of it. Get it right and it will set the tone for all routines to follow. It will set the tone for effort, behavior, and academic performance too.

This doesn't mean, however, that you're going to be a demanding ogre. Be sure you teach with a spirit of fun and confidence. Routines can be drudgery if you drill them like an old football coach.

All Model

Once you feel confident your students can do the routine individually, then send your entire class outside with their backpacks to perform the routine simultaneously. Emphasize politeness as they work around each other to hang up hats and maneuver around desks. "Good morning," "please," and "excuse me" should be the predominant communication during the opening routine.

You're only job during this time is to observe, saying as little as possible. Resist the urge to talk them through the routine—which will weaken rather than strengthen performance and create dependency on you. Let them do it on their own. Give them a chance to mature and grow and test themselves. It builds confidence and competence, and their body language will show it.

When they finish, if they get it right, be sure and tell them that it's perfect, that it can't be done any better. Many teachers are afraid to do this. They've been led to believe that no one ever arrives, that there is always more to learn. But it isn't true. Once they prove they can do it well, then heartily let them know it.

Note: Although you'll want to practice until they get it right, it's okay to take a break and revisit the routine later in the day—or the next. Repetition, after all, isn't a bad word.

It Starts Now

Teaching a highly detailed routine to perfection on the first day of school is the single best thing you can do to ensure a well-behaved and productive school year. It sets the standard for every routine, lesson, and activity to follow. It raises the bar of what is normal from mediocrity to excellence.

It sends the message that your new students are now part of something special, something different, something bigger and more important than themselves. And they'll love it. It feels good. It fills them with purpose and drive. It motivates and inspires. It alights a fire of intrinsic motivation to listen, to learn, to behave, and to enjoy being a member of your classroom.

You are not every teacher, and yours isn't any old classroom. You *can* have the dream class you want. You can have the teaching experience you envisioned when you first decided to become a teacher. But it starts here. It starts now. It starts with this simple 20-minute lesson.

3

How a One-Second Strategy
Can Motivate Your New Class

FOR YEARS I'VE HAD a poster on my classroom door that reads "Learn Like A Champion Today." Each student taps it on their way in. To an outsider it may appear to be a silly ritual. Cutesy, perhaps, but of no real consequence.

They would be wrong.

In fact, I believe it to be an important motivational tool. Granted, by itself, the poster doesn't mean much. It's a homemade 12" x 18" rectangle of laminated construction paper. But the act of tapping it, the decision to reach up and give it a rap, is where you'll find its power.

It's the meaning behind the action that makes it work. Tapping the poster is a way of saying yes to you, your program, and the learning environment you've created. It's a physical expression of their commitment *before* they even enter your classroom.

It also serves as a reminder that hard work, good behavior, and politeness are expected. But you can't just slap it up on your door and expect it to have an effect. You must first define its meaning. You must walk your students outside your classroom during the first week of school and, while modeling how you want them to enter, explain that by tapping the poster they're agreeing to three things:

1. To give their best.
2. To behave their best.
3. To have a positive attitude.

These aren't rules, mind you. They're a set of principles that define the learning culture you want to create. So when a student taps it, they're in effect buying into that culture.

Further, tapping the poster flips an internal switch, signaling that it's time for school and that negativity, laziness, immaturity, and the like must be left outside the door. The result is that they enter your room ready to learn.

Again, it's the meaning the poster represents that makes this so. It's the promise and commitment that comes with the decision to tap it that elicits the Pavlovian-like response. So what happens if they don't tap it? What if they stroll by without so much as a glance at the poster? Nothing at all. *Because it must be entirely their choice.* If it isn't, if you force your students to tap it or glare at them when they don't, then it loses its power. It no longer possesses any meaning. But here's the thing: As long as your students enjoy being part of your class it will become a habit they enthusiastically take part in.

You may be thinking, *Well, that's fine and good for some teachers, but the students at my school are too jaded (or too old or too cool).* I haven't found this to be the case. In fact, the more challenging the school, the more impactful the strategy.

The idea is a play on a poster the Notre Dame and University of Oklahoma football teams tap on their way out to the field.

And if 85 young men from every conceivable background can buy in, so can your class.

It's important to note that the poster isn't a panacea. On its own, it can't make or break your classroom. It's merely a strategy that supports a happy and well-behaved learning environment. It's a strategy that helps ensure that each day begins on the right foot, that each day starts with a reminder that entering your classroom comes with responsibility. The next 60 minutes, or six hours, *matters*, and so do they.

4

How to Build Rapport on the First Day of School

B
UILDING RAPPORT IS ONE of an umbrella of strategies whose goal is to create a classroom your students love being part of. And why is that important? Because when your students look forward to your class, *everything* is easier. From behavior to attentiveness to work habits, every area of classroom management is made better.

But you must start on the first day of school. You must start when your students are eager and most receptive. You must start the moment they enter your classroom.

Here's how:

Greet

Stand at your classroom door and personally say hello to every student as they walk in. Look them in the eye, ask them their name, and then introduce yourself. It's well worth the few minutes. The giving, respectful nature of the gesture makes an immediate impact and will prompt them to reciprocate respect and kindness right back at you.

Smile

The oft-recommended advice that you should never smile the first month of the school year is nonsense. In fact, smiling generously on the very first day is a great way to build rapport. It makes you instantly likable. It puts your students at ease. It wins them over to your way of doing things before you even open your mouth.

Share

It's important on the first day of school for your students to see you as a real person, and not a robot built by the government to tell them what to do. A quick and easy way to do this is to share a story about your childhood. Shoot for something funny or amusing, perhaps about your own first day of school experience. Nothing builds rapport faster.

Laugh

No, you don't have to tell riotous jokes or be knee-slapping funny. Just be open to sharing a laugh with your new class. Humor is everywhere and your spontaneous enjoyment of it will increase your likability tenfold. It will cause your students to want to get to know you, listen to you, and behave for you. It makes your sky-high expectations of them not only go down a lot smoother, but be readily, eagerly fulfilled.

Promise

We have talked about the importance of promising to follow your classroom management plan. But it's also important to promise your students that your personality will remain consistent. So before your first classroom management lesson, tell them directly. Promise that you will never yell or speak to them disrespectfully. It's a simple statement, but so, so powerful—for both them and you.

Game-Changers

The rapport-building strategies above are simple, wee little gestures, barely registering on your effort meter. But combined with a pin-neat room environment and detailed teaching of rules, consequences, and routines, they're game-changers.

They create leverage and influence, instant likability and leadership presence. They make your immovable boundary lines of behavior *matter* to students. They build an immediate relationship, engender trust and respect, and fill your students with the confidence that with you at the helm anything is possible.

Your students will exit your classroom excited to tell their parents how much they love their new teacher and can't wait to get to school the next day. You'll just smile and wave. And as you close the door on the first day of school, you'll breathe easy, quietly triumphant. Because you've just set the tone for the best year of teaching you've ever had.

5

Why You Shouldn't Let Your Students Decide the Class Rules

ALLOWING STUDENTS TO COME up with the class rules is a common strategy. And at first glance, it appears to be a good one. But dig deeper into the whys and hows of effective classroom management, and you'll discover it to be a mistake.

The idea behind the strategy is to provide students with a sense of ownership by guiding them through the construction of class rules you already have in mind. If you trust them with this important part of your classroom structure, the argument goes, they'll be more likely to buy into your classroom management plan. They'll be more likely to feel a sense of responsibility and less likely to dismiss, reject, or complain about rules they themselves came up with. So what's not to like?

Well, the problem with the strategy is that it can undermine your leadership presence. It can negatively affect how your students see you and your role as their teacher. You see, if in any way you communicate that you're in partnership with your students when determining the direction of your classroom, it will weaken your authority.

They'll view you not as a confident leader who knows what is best for them and their education, but as an unsure cohort who makes suggestions they can either take or leave. This, in turn, can make enforcing your rules significantly more difficult. It will increase the likelihood of arguments over what does and doesn't constitute breaking them. It will cause a reluctance to go to time-out—or an outright refusal—rather than an acceptance of wrongdoing. Your students will be *less* likely to take responsibility and more likely to sulk, complain, or blame you for holding them accountable.

The unintended message students receive by taking part in creating the very boundaries of your classroom is that everything is negotiable, which then opens the floodgates to debate on matters that should only be decided by you. This view of teacher as partner tends to be especially problematic with difficult students, who are quick to fill any void you leave them. Unless you establish yourself as the clear leader from the get-go, they'll spend the year trying to wrest control from you.

Having a teacher students trust to be at the helm from morning bell to dismissal has a calming effect on the tone and tenor of your classroom. It allows your students to relax, enjoy school, and concentrate on learning. This isn't to say that they should never be given the opportunity to make decisions. You can still encourage a sense of ownership by letting your students vote on matters unrelated to the course and direction of your classroom.

Do you want to play this math game or that one?
Do you want to give your presentations before or after lunch?
Do you want to do the lesson inside or outside on the grass?

There are dozens of opportunities to allow students to make decisions that don't interfere with your role and position as their teacher. The truth is, you and your students have distinctly different responsibilities. Problems large and small arise when those responsibilities become confused or intertwined.

By presenting your rules as non-negotiable boundaries that *you put into place* for the express purpose of protecting their right to learn and enjoy school, you establish yourself as a compassionate leader who puts their interests first. You establish yourself as a leader worth following.

How to Be Consistent From the First Day of School to the Last

THERE IS GREAT FREEDOM in consistency. Because when you follow your classroom management plan to a tee, you remove the guesswork. You eliminate the stress of lecturing, correcting, and trying to convince your students to behave. You wipe away the friction and resentment.

The responsibility for misbehavior, then, falls entirely on them—with none of it clinging to you. Your students are free to reflect on their mistakes, and you're free to move on as if nothing happened.

A Slippery Slope

It's common for teachers to begin the school year determined to be consistent. But somewhere along the line they lose their way. They get distracted and let minor misbehavior go. They look the other way when crunched for time. They take misbehavior personally, become angry, and deliver a dressing-down instead.

Before long they're enforcing rules based on their mood, who the student is, or the severity of the misbehavior rather than what their plan actually says. Which leads to distrust, animosity, and more and more misbehavior.

Unfortunately, it's so, so easy to ski down this slippery slope and so, so difficult to find your way back up.

One Thing

There is, however, one simple thing you can do on the first day of school to make sure you stay consistent throughout the year. It's a strategy that makes following your classroom management plan something you do naturally, even effortlessly. It becomes automatic, like opening the door when an expected guest knocks or answering the phone when it rings.

It isn't, however, for the fainthearted, for it entails going on record, making a commitment, and putting your reputation at stake.

The Promise

The way the strategy works is that on the very first day of school, within the first hour, you're going to make an ironclad promise. You're going to make a promise to your class that you will follow your classroom management plan precisely as it's written. No exceptions.

It will come while you're introducing your plan and be repeated during every subsequent classroom management lesson as you teach, model, and practice the ins and outs of your rules and consequences. *"I promise that I will protect your right to learn and enjoy school by following our classroom management plan every time a rule is broken."* Pause, look them in the eyes, then say it again. Keep on saying it every day until doing it becomes second nature to you, until you've proven to yourself and your class that you are indeed a person of your word.

All In

Teachers are quick to ask students to make promises regarding their behavior, even asking for them to be written out and signed.

But the real power is when the teacher makes a promise. Because when you publicly state your intention and commitment, you create powerful internal leverage to actually do it. Even when it's inconvenient. Even when you're rushed. Even when the storm of the century is raging outside your classroom door.

By putting yourself on notice and holding yourself accountable for doing what you say you're going to do, being consistent becomes remarkably easy. In no time you'll be someone your students know they can trust and count on, maybe for the first time in their life. You'll become someone worth looking up to and following and behaving for.

So go all in. Lay it on the line within the first moments you meet your new class. And the soft pressure to honor your promise, to do the right thing, to ensure your students the best learning experience they've ever had . . . will never, ever leave you.

7

Why You Should Take Your Time the First Few Weeks of School

NO MATTER WHAT YOU hear from your colleagues, no matter how far they say they've gotten into the curriculum, or how they're already working in groups or rotating students through centers, avoid the temptation to join them. Avoid rushing to catch up. Avoid pushing your students along too fast. Avoid comparing yourself or judging yourself or stressing out over what anyone else is doing.

Because in just a few short weeks, when your fellow teachers are complaining about the pressure and the stress, about the misbehavior and how far they've fallen behind, you'll be singing a different tune.

It pays, you see, to get it right the first time around. It pays to take a deliberate approach, to teach the details, the ins and outs, and the A to Zs of being a polite, successful, and contributing member of your classroom.

In the beginning your students' eagerness to do well can mask the reality that they're unprepared to hit the ground running, unprepared to fully transition to their new grade level, and unprepared for your Everest-like expectations. This is why, even if you teach, model, and rehearse your routines thoroughly, they can surprise you with how poorly they put them into practice.

For example, let's say you're walking your students to lunch. You leave your room in a calm, brisk-moving line. As you approach sight of the lunchroom, your students are rolling along precisely as modeled. You couldn't be happier with how well they're performing the routine.

But then, unexpectedly, other classes join you in the hallway. The line backs up. All heck breaks loose.

You watch aghast as your students begin stepping out of line to goof and jostle with their friends, shout out to little brothers or big sisters, and disrupt the working classrooms lining the hallway. If you're to be honest, their behavior is, in a word, embarrassing. It's easy in such situations to get discouraged, to overreact, and to question both your classroom management ability and the potential of your new class.

But you would be wrong on both counts. Because early in the school year an occasional breakdown in behavior is *expected*. No teacher escapes the first few weeks without being tested, tried, or disappointed. How you handle it is what separates exceptional teachers from the rest.

So when something like this happens, when you have a bad moment while on your way to lunch or the wheels fall off during read aloud or every last one of your students runs on the way out to recess, it isn't the end of the world. It doesn't mean you have a bad class. It doesn't mean you're not a good teacher. And it doesn't mean that you should forgo your expectations of excellence or lower the bar on what you know is best for them and their future.

Rather, when your students take a misstep—or flat out ignore your directives—it's an opportunity to show them that you really do mean what you say. It's an opportunity to prove to them that you're a leader worth following. It's an opportunity to back up, take a deep breath, and get it right. Once you convince your class that when you say it they can take it to the bank, *everything* becomes easier.

So slow down. Take your time. Show them what a good student looks like. Show them how you expect them to listen to instruction, dismiss to recess, turn in work, meet in groups, ask a question, line up for lunch, and even how to have fun. And if you have a bad moment, if your students fail to meet your standards, keep your cool, observe closely, and wait until you can be alone with your class before addressing what you saw and how it strayed from your teaching.

Hold them to it and they'll learn. Take them back to the scene of the crime and give them a chance to fix it and they will. Accept nothing less than their best, and they'll give it to you.

8

How to Handle a Class That Tests You Right From the Get-Go

YOU BEGIN THE SCHOOL year with so much hope. But then, not an hour after teaching your classroom management plan, your students are misbehaving. They're talking when you're talking. They're leaving their seats without permission. They're calling out, giggling, and ignoring your directions.

It's disheartening—and only natural to feel as if you did something wrong. It's only natural to think that maybe you weren't clear enough, maybe you didn't model with enough detail or communicate with enough conviction. And although these can be significant factors in how quickly and eagerly students respond to your behavior expectations, it doesn't mean that all hope is lost. Not even close. It isn't unusual to be tested upon first introducing your classroom management plan. At some schools, and with some students, it's even expected—no matter how thorough you teach your plan.

So if it happens to you, there is no need to panic. In fact, your first response should be to do absolutely nothing. Don't jump in and try to stop the misbehavior. Don't raise your voice or show your frustration. Don't even try to enforce consequences. Just wait. Breathe. Observe. Smile inwardly—because you're going to fix it.

It's important to mention that if behavior is poor from the get-go, it doesn't mean that you're going to have a bad year. It just means that your students don't believe that you're really going to do what you say. Perhaps it's because you're a new teacher or at a new school. Perhaps their previous teacher or teachers were inconsistent and had poor classroom management skills. Perhaps you're a bit nervous, tentative, and not quite sure of yourself—and your students can sense it. No matter. None of it is predictive of a stressful or unsuccessful year. Nor is it anything to get overly concerned about. *It's what you do in response that's important.*

Most teachers will try to enforce consequences as fast as they can, but this is a mistake with a large group of misbehaving students because it risks inciting aggressive and disrespectful pushback. It's also incredibly stressful and puts you at odds with your new class. Getting angry and taking it personally, too, is a mistake that will undermine your ability to take back control and begin creating a well-behaved class.

No, it's best just to keep your cool and watch. Let them notice you waiting unconcerned. Give it a few minutes, and in all likelihood, they'll begin to settle down and look your way. If they don't, however, if they're hell-bent on continuing to disrupt, then calmly and kindly begin shooing them to their seats while repeating a request for quiet attention.

The idea is to *gently* guide them from chaos and excitability to calm and agreeable. Keep your voice soft and maintain an even keel. Continue in this vein of guiding and requesting until they're *generally* quiet and looking in your direction. Then, without explanation, immediately jump into reteaching your classroom management plan as if for the first time.

If they complain, ignore it. Do not engage in discussion or debate about what are your responsibilities as the leader of the class. Your classroom management plan, and the rules and consequences that govern it, isn't negotiable.

This time, though, when you teach your plan, you must do it with far greater boldness and determination. You must find the strength within to give it all you've got. Ramp up the detail, the clarity, and the *passion*.

This is your career, after all, and you're going to be with this class for the next nine months. So teach your plan in a way that signals to every student that you're no ordinary teacher and yours is no ordinary classroom. Remove any doubt that they're going to be held accountable for every rule transgression. Model, playact, and emote what breaking rules looks and feels like. Let them visualize the experience. Walk your students through the precise steps a misbehaving student would take from warning to parent contact. Teach the heck out of it, leaving nothing to chance and nothing to misunderstand. *Because the way you teach your classroom management plan matters.*

You mustn't be intimidated or fearful. Exceptional classroom management, especially with a tough class, takes courage. And if you're not feeling confident, if your heart is beating out of your chest and your palms are sweaty, *then fake it.* Pretend you have all the power and confidence you need to have the exact class you want. Believe. Trust. Take a leap of faith, and *they will respond.*

After checking for understanding through questioning, practice, and/or role-play—which can vary depending on grade level—you're ready to begin holding them accountable. If, however, a few days later it happens again—more than a few students are misbehaving and you're feeling as if you're losing control—then cancel whatever lesson or activity you have planned and teach your classroom management plan again. And if need be, again.

Teach it until they "get it." Teach it until they know that rebelling is futile. Teach it until they can't wait to show you how well they can follow it. Never, ever accept less than what is best for your students, their education, and their future. Be the teacher they need. And they'll be the class you want.

9

Why You Should Ignore Difficult Students the First Week of School

N O, YOU'RE NOT GOING to ignore their misbehavior. It's just that . . . well, let's back up a little. When you first receive your roster for the coming year, it's normal to want to get the lowdown on your new class. It's normal to seek out teachers from the grade below to see if you have any especially difficult students. This isn't necessarily a bad thing. But by doing so, you can actually *trigger* their misbehavior. You can cause these challenging students to jump right back into the same bad habits they struggled with the year before.

You see, teachers who know ahead of time which students have a proclivity to misbehave will inevitably try to nip it in the bud. They'll try to prevent it from growing into a major problem. So they'll seat them in the front of the room. They'll pull them aside for pep-talks, warnings, and reminders. They'll try to "catch them doing good" and use their hovering presence as a deterrent.

But what this does is send the message that nothing has changed from the year before—or the year before that. Teacher after teacher have employed the same strategies. Yet they continue to disrupt learning. They continue to be silly. They continue to argue, play around, and get up and wander the room during lessons. Because the extra attention, especially during the first week of school, is a form of labeling.

It tells them loud and clear that they're not like the other students. It tells them that they're not good enough, that they can't control themselves, and that they need special attention. The truth is, labeling has a profound effect on individual behavior, *more so than any other classroom variable*. It reinforces the false narrative difficult students already believe about themselves that "behavior problem" *is* who they are—as much a part of them as their eye color or shoe size.

So, on the first day of school, when they find their assigned seat in the front of the room, when they notice your frequent and proximate attention, when they're asked to line up behind the most well-behaved student in the class . . . their heart sinks. Because they know that no matter what—new year, new class, new teacher—they can't escape their destiny. Resigned to their fate, they shrug their shoulders and give you *exactly* what you expect. They become a walking, talking, misbehaving self-fulfilling prophecy. It's sad and tragic. Yet it's a scenario that is repeated again and again in classrooms all over the world, with the same predictable results.

From the moment the new school year begins, if your behavior is in any way different around those few students with a "reputation," they'll recognize it immediately. After all, they're looking for it. They're highly attuned to it. They know it intimately because they've been on the receiving end of it their entire lives. So what should you do instead? Treat them with the same gentle kindness, humor, and respect you do all of your students.

Don't go out of your way. Don't seat them in front of the room. Don't pull them aside for reminders, if-I-were-yous, false praises, warnings, and the like. Instead, give them a chance to turn over a new leaf.

Pretend they're already perfectly well behaved. Act as if they're already successful. Show them that you believe in them by interacting with them just like you do everyone else. Give them hope that this year is going to be different, and those backbreaking labels, which are causing so much of their misbehavior, will begin to slide off their shoulders. Their eyes will rise to meet yours. Their expressions will soften. Their breathing will deepen. Relief will wash over them like a summer rain. Again, this doesn't mean that you'll ignore their misbehavior. You'll still follow your classroom management plan to the letter. You'll still hold them accountable. Just like everyone else.

Give these school weary and teacher wary students a chance to become the potential you see in them. Grant them a new prophecy. Rewrite their story. And they'll never be the same.

10

How to Improve Classroom Management Every Day

ONE OF THE SECRETS to exceptional classroom management is to aim for the stars. It's to accept nothing less than what you want for your classroom, your students, and your career. It doesn't matter where you teach. It doesn't matter who is on your roster. It doesn't matter if chaos and disorder reign supreme in the hallways of your school.

If you have a vision, and the right tools, you can take *any* group of students and transform them into the class you desire. You can have peace, a safe haven, a sanctuary of learning within the four walls of your classroom. At SCM, we hear from teachers every week who have done just that. Anyone can do it.

But you mustn't settle for just okay. You mustn't merely hope to keep a lid on your classroom. You mustn't wish for just a *little* better. Effective classroom management doesn't work that way. To have the well-behaved class you want, you have to push your students to get better every day. One easy way to do that is with a strategy that I call "The List."

The way it works is that you're going to keep a short daily list of the routines, behaviors, and activities that were done perfectly as well as a list of the areas that need work. Logistically, I recommend keeping a single sheet of paper on the same clipboard you use to keep track of consequences.

On the top half of the page, jot down what went well. In other words, what expectations were fulfilled exactly as they were taught? So, if your students were fully engaged during literature circles, for example, or if their attention was spot-on during your instruction, then write it down.

On the bottom half of the page, make note of anything that didn't go according to what you expressly taught to your students. If you had to redo a routine or reteach an expectation, if you observed off-task behavior or directions that were semi-followed (or not followed at all), you would add it to the bottom list.

This isn't something you have to do immediately. You can even wait until the end of the day. But the next morning, first thing, you're going to pull out your list and share it with your students. You may say something like:

> *"Quickly, I wanted to mention that I thought you were excellent during literature circles yesterday. The discussions were interesting and in-depth. I heard some great ideas. Everyone was involved and participating the whole period. Also, your focus and attention during the science lesson was especially good. I don't expect any better than that. Well done."*

Then move to the bottom list:

> *"Some areas we need to improve . . . Yesterday, when I gave the signal to line up for lunch, there was some bumping and pushing, which is why we had to do it over again. Today, I expect it to be done correctly. There was also talking during*

independent work time, and those students received a consequence. Today, let's be sure to give everyone a chance to concentrate on their work without disruption."

And that's it, very simple. You won't add a lecture. You won't threaten or feign disappointment. You won't over-praise, raise your voice, or give anything but the unvarnished truth. What you are doing, however, is providing feedback.

Feedback, in the form of letting students know directly and honestly how they're doing, and if what they're doing is, indeed, how you taught them, is a little-known key to effective classroom management.

It works because it reinforces their understanding of where your standard is. It further illuminates the proper path and gives them something to improve upon every day. It moves your class closer and closer to your dream destination—until the bottom list all but disappears.

The list strategy is a tangible way of keeping score, of knowing how you're doing, of communicating to your students where you're headed and what being a good student and an exceptional classroom looks like. There is deep pride in doing things well, in seeing evidence of progress, in getting better every day through the pursuit of excellence. No matter who your students are or how jaded they appear, it's highly, endlessly motivational. It's intrinsic and pure. It keeps the momentum rolling, the pedal to the metal.

The goal within reach.

PART TWO:
Accountability

II

I Stopped Holding My Students Accountable and Here Is What Happened

S O I RAN THIS experiment. And enough time has passed that I can now share it with you. Here's what happened:

I was halfway through the semester with a class I really enjoyed. I had prepared them well to start the year by employing the same strategies I teach at here at SCM. And it showed. They were polite and well behaved. They were independent and listened well. We were cruising along, and I couldn't have been happier.

But for the sake of knowledge, and for a deeper understanding of what many teachers face every day, I thought I'd try something interesting. For one week, I decided to no longer rely on my classroom management plan. That's right. I just stopped following it. I didn't change who I was or how I interacted with students. I didn't raise my voice or begin glaring and lecturing. I just stopped holding them accountable.

So when a few students began whispering to each other while I was giving instruction, which was the first misbehavior I noticed, I just paused and smiled or gently asked them to stop. But that was it. I continued in this manner as more rule breaking began popping up. This wasn't a surprise. Remove accountability and it's bound to happen sooner rather than later.

But what I wasn't prepared for, and found most curious, was that my relationship with my students quickly began to change. By Wednesday morning, it was clear that their opinion of me had dropped a few notches. They no longer looked at me the same way. They weren't as friendly or as pleased to see me. Some hardly made eye contact and nearly all were markedly slower to listen and follow my directions. I started to feel like the invisible man.

Although they were never out of control or outright rude and disrespectful, I could feel the animosity building. Toward the end of the week, I was coaxing and cajoling them through lessons and all but tap dancing to keep their attention. I ramped up the engagement and overt friendliness, but could still feel control of the class slipping away. My leverage and influence was fading before my eyes and my leadership presence was fading before theirs.

They, in turn, began showing signs of frustration and discontent. They grumbled under their breath and expelled sigh after sigh, all over the room. Their enthusiasm waned and they slumped lower and lower in their seats. I was working in a challenging school, mind you, but it became clear that my simple kindness and good humor alone weren't enough to stem the downward tide. They needed accountability as their counterpoint.

One thing I found especially interesting about the experiment, and heartening, frankly, was that as the week went on more and more students approached me to ask variations of, *"What are you doing?" "Why are you doing this?"* and *"Are you okay?"* By Friday morning, I decided that enough was enough and came clean about the experiment. They were relieved, to say the least. Many laughed and said that they knew something was up. Some even mentioned that they had been worried about me.

After a quick review of the rules and consequences, and promising never to do it again, things went back to normal almost immediately. Blessed peace returned to the kingdom.

That afternoon, I asked them to write about their experiences. We shared out in groups and as a class. It was a great lesson in the value of firm boundaries—and not just in class, but in society and in their own personal lives. They came away with a deeper understanding of how and why a fair, consistently followed classroom management plan is for *them*, not the teacher.

They learned in a memorable way that it's the very thing that ensures their right to learn and enjoy school, that it safeguards them from disruption and frees them to focus on their responsibilities. They also learned just how profoundly even minor misbehavior can affect others as well as the entire mood of the class.

Fair, every-single-time accountability is a powerful force for good. It's a wonderful benefit for students and indispensable to creating a happy and well-behaved class. If you're anything less than fully committed, consistent, and faithful to your classroom management plan, then double down on it today. Take a stand for your students. Make a promise to yourself and to them that you will follow it exactly as it's written.

12

3 Big Mistakes Teachers Make
When Enforcing Consequences

B EING CONSISTENT WITH YOUR classroom management plan is especially important to begin the school year.
This alone will go a long way toward creating the learning
environment you really want. Once you've conquered this challenge, however, there is another pitfall looming around the corner.

You see, *how* you enforce your plan in no small part deter-
mines how effective it will be. Get it wrong and you risk nullifying
the many benefits of being consistent. Get it right and it's smooth
sailing. What follows are three big mistakes teachers make when
enforcing consequences. You'll do well to avoid them.

1. Showing displeasure.

It's normal to occasionally feel disappointment or frustration when
a student misbehaves, particularly if it interrupts the class. But you
must never show outward signs of it. Sighing, glaring, frowning,
and the like create friction and animosity, which takes the focus
off the student and their misbehavior and makes it a personal
feud between you. So instead of reflecting on their misbehavior,
taking responsibility for it, and vowing to never do it again, they'll
grumble under their breath and seethe in anger at you.

2. Waiting for a response.

Another common mistake is to enforce a consequence and then wait for a response. Most teachers do this because they want the student to verbally answer for their misbehavior. But this isn't what your classroom management plan says.

Further, waiting for an explanation—or coming right out and asking the student why they misbehaved—is an invitation to argue. It provides an opening for the student to justify for their misbehavior, point the finger elsewhere, or try to convince you that you didn't see what you just saw. It's also a stressful and monumental waste of time.

3. Adding your two cents.

The final big mistake usually crops up when the teacher decides to escort the student to time-out—which is a no-no. It may also come later while checking on the student in time-out. Instead of allowing the consequence to work, the teacher will express their disappointment in the student. They'll tell them how they should feel, what they should think, and how they should behave the next time. But this interferes with the student coming to these conclusions on their own, which can be a powerful experience and the very point of time-out.

How to Enforce

Enforcing consequences effectively is a quick and painless process. As soon as you witness misbehavior, calmly approach the offending student, look them in the eye, and deliver your line:

"You have a warning because you broke rule number two and left your seat without raising your hand." Then turn and walk away.

When a student misbehaves, your only job is to inform. It's to hold them accountable in the least disruptive way so your classroom management plan can do its good work. This way, you safeguard your relationship with the student. You allow them to ponder their mistake and take responsibility for it. You empower them to learn, mature, and leave their misbehavior behind them.

13

Why You Should Never Punish Your Entire Class for the Behavior of a Few

A FRIEND EMAILED ME TO share a story about his son's first week of school. Evidently, some of his classmates were misbehaving, and in response the teacher kept the entire class in for recess. This isn't an unusual strategy. I often hear from teachers asking if they should do the same. At first glance it seems like an odd question with an obvious answer. But the truth is, keeping everyone in for recess, taking away points, or asking them to put their heads down can indeed get unruly students temporarily under control. It's a reliable way to get the class quiet and settled down. It gives the teacher a much-needed breather and usually results in calmer behavior for the next lesson.

The problem with the strategy, however, is that it alienates your most well-behaved students.

When my friend's son got home after school he was angry and confused. It didn't make sense to him. Why did he have to stay in for recess when he did nothing wrong? Why indeed?

Students from kindergarten on up have an acute sense of fairness. Although they may not always voice their frustration to you, you can bet they'll bring it up at the dinner table. You can bet they'll look at you differently. Holding everyone accountable when only a few are misbehaving creates resentment and will damage your influence.

This begs the question, then, of redoing routines, which I recommend. Isn't asking your entire class to repeat a routine a form of holding everyone accountable? Yes, it is. But there are some notable differences. First, you should never redo a routine if the problem is just a few students. This underscores the importance of closely observing all routines and then being quick to enforce individual consequences. This alone virtually guarantees that it will never be more than one or two students.

Also, when you redo a routine, it's not because of misbehavior. It's because your class did the routine incorrectly. It's because they didn't quite believe that when you taught the routine so explicitly, you actually meant it. Furthermore, after now 29 years of teaching students in kindergarten through high school, a poorly performed routine is usually, almost exclusively, *everyone*. And although we often use the word 'redoing,' it's best to think of it as reteaching. Even if you're not actually modeling the routine again, asking your class to show you how you expect them to do it is a form of reteaching. It's a way to communicate that when you say something, you mean it.

Finally, when you ask students to repeat a routine, you're not taking anything away from them. They aren't missing recess or arriving late to lunch or losing out on class points. You're merely backing your words with action and ensuring what is best for them and their learning.

To sum up, when individual students misbehave, hold them accountable individually by following your classroom management plan. If it's more than one or two at a time, then it's a sign you must become a more vigilant observer. When the class as a whole performs a routine poorly, have them do it again as a form of reteaching. In this way, you'll never alienate students, cause resentment, or feel the need to punish everyone for the behavior of a few.

14

Why You Should Never Give Choices Instead of Consequences

A T SCM, WE HEAR from teachers and administrators from all four corners of the globe, and one of the more perplexing trends in classroom management is to give students choices instead of consequences.

For example, let's say a student named Jason is up and walking about your room while the rest of the class is working independently. He's tapping his pencil on various objects. He's shuffling his feet. And although capable, he's grumbling under his breath that he doesn't want to do his work anymore. But instead of simply giving him a warning for breaking a class rule, you negotiate with him. You try to coax him away from disturbing others by giving him options to choose from.

> *"Hey Jase, do you want to do just a few problems instead of all of them?"*
> *"How 'bout if you did your work on the rug? Would you like that?"*
> *"Would you prefer to draw a picture instead of writing it out?"*
> *"Why don't you take a little break and work on your iPad?"*

"What about taking a walk down the hall, and getting away for a few minutes?"
"Do you want to be my helper, and do your work another time?"

You get the picture. The idea is to remove the source of his discontentment, to entice him with alternatives so that he will no longer engage in unwanted behavior. And as long as you're willing to go far enough (*"Hey, do you want to sit in my chair?"*), the strategy will work. It will indeed stop him from disrupting the class. No doubt about it. So what's not to like?

Well, as poet Elizabeth Barrett Browning once wrote, "Let me count the ways."

1. When you appease difficult students by lowering academic or behavioral standards, you send an unmistakable message that they can complain, disrupt, and misbehave their way out of anything they deem unpleasant.

2. Offering choices rewards bad behavior, defiance, selfishness, and the like, thus encouraging more frequent and more severe misbehavior. Unless, that is, you continue lowering the bar and sweetening the choices.

3. By giving in so readily, even voluntarily, you're essentially telling them that you believe they're incapable of changing their behavior. This is a form of labeling, and it is devastating to difficult students.

4. It's confirmation from an authoritative source that misbehavior isn't just something they do, but it's who they are, like eye color or shoe size, and something they have little control over. Unless this label is reversed, they will continue to misbehave year after year.

5. It's a philosophy that believes that an upset or uncomfortable child is to be avoided at all costs, which not only doesn't reflect the world we live in, but it makes a mockery of the critical role of perseverance and hard work in academic as well as personal success.

6. Offering choices assuages misbehavior in the moment, but does nothing to curb it going forward. In other words, it's a band-aid that sacrifices the child's future for the here and now.

7. When you excuse, enable, and offer escape routes, you set limits on students and their capacity to rise above challenges and overcome difficulties. You lead them away from success, not toward it.

8. Letting students off the hook is akin to telling them they're not good enough or worthy enough to be held to a higher standard, which strips away dignity and self-confidence faster and more effectively than yelling, sarcasm, or any other harmful method.

9. Going back on your word by failing to follow the rules of your classroom causes resentment and distrust from

all students and severely limits your ability to lead and build meaningful, influential relationships.

10. Baiting students with more attractive choices creates an environment of entitlement and causes them to react to firm direction and accountability with aggressive push-back.

Yes, They Can

It is possible to temporarily placate difficult students into better behavior. But the cost is their very future. It's a shameful strategy that hands leverage and control over to students who frankly don't know what's best for them. Our job is to teach our students how to overcome obstacles, not avoid them with excuses and manipulation.

When you offer choices in exchange for *not* disrupting the class, when you lighten the workload and remove responsibility, you are in every sense giving up on them. You are in every sense telling them that they're not worth holding accountable.

As a result, they come to believe that they're weak-minded and incapable of improvement, incapable of sitting, listening, and learning, and incapable of being anything other than the court jester your words and actions suggest. It's tragic and demeaning and so, so sad.

The truth is, no matter how difficult a student's home life, no matter how tough they have it, or how emotional and angry they can get when things don't go their way, you do them no favors by letting them off the hook. You do them no favors by giving in, making excuses, or offering a bunny hill when the rest of the class is testing themselves on Kilimanjaro.

So what's the alternative? You follow your classroom management plan. You let accountability and your undying belief in them do their good work. You let the hard lessons that are part of every well-lived life embolden them to become better, more resilient, and more capable than they themselves ever thought possible. In other words, instead of offering choices and telling them they can't, give them consequences and tell them they can.

15

Why Giving a "Look" Is a Poor Classroom Management Strategy

T'S A POPULAR STRATEGY. You notice two students talking and giggling during a lesson, for example, so you move into their field of vision and give them "the look." You deliver the old evil eye. You communicate with your piercing stare and tight lips that you dislike what they're doing, that they better cut it out, or else.

Now, this may indeed stop them from continuing to disrupt your lesson. The problem, however, is that the strategy causes more misbehavior in the future.

Here's why:

It's antagonistic.

Whenever you glare at students, or otherwise try to intimidate them into behaving, you create a you-against-them relationship. You make it personal. You give the impression that not only are you angry, but you dislike them personally.

After all, when someone gives a dirty look, that's the natural conclusion—especially with children. It causes private hurt and resentment and ultimately results in you having less influence over their behavior choices.

It's confusing.

When you give a "look," you have no way of knowing whether your students understand what it means. They may not even be sure you're looking at them or what behavior you're referring to. Short of saying, "Hey Emily, I gave you that look earlier because you weren't on task," chances are they'll be confused.

Effective classroom management requires you to communicate clearly with your students, to tell them directly how they transgressed the rules and what will happen as a result.

Note: In *The Smart Classroom Management Plan for High School Teachers,* which is available on the SCM website, we recommend eye contact as one of two defined ways of giving a warning, which is altogether different than giving a "look."

It's inconsistent.

When you promise to follow your classroom management plan, but then go back on your word and glare instead, you send the message that you can't be trusted.

Furthermore, the use of intimidation, no matter how mild it seems in the moment, isn't accountability. It doesn't result in students taking responsibility or vowing to do better in the future. It just makes them angry and emboldened to misbehave behind your back. A leader worth following is someone who does what they say they're going to do.

No Friction

Giving a "look" is another in a long line of strategies that can curb misbehavior in the moment, but that make classroom management more difficult down the line. Sadly, this strategy is recommended by more than a few educational "experts." It's passed around as a viable solution because, by golly, it gets Robert back on track. But now Robert can't stand his teacher and has little motivation to push himself academically.

To create a peaceful learning environment that frees you to be the inspiring and influential teacher you were meant to be, you must be able to hold your students accountable without causing friction. You must follow your classroom management plan as it is written and give them an opportunity to take responsibility all on their own—without your dirty looks, lectures, or two cents.

In this way, you maintain your likability and influence. You safeguard your relationships. You create a world that makes sense, a world your students love being part of, a world where you can teach without disruption.

16

Why Kindness Is a Powerful Classroom Management Strategy

CONSISTENT ACCOUNTABILITY COMBINED WITH a kindhearted nature results in a nicer, friendlier class. They work together to rid your classroom of incivility and disrespect. They turn what you thought and feared were most disagreeable students into the lovely people you wish them to be.

For many teachers, the change can be quite startling, even perplexing. *"My gosh, Joshua is so nice to me now. I never thought he could be so polite."* But it's nothing of the sort. In fact, it's highly predictable and steeped in human nature.

You see, students are accustomed to having anger and frustration attached to accountability. They're used to teachers enforcing consequences with an air of revenge or reciprocity. It may be subtle, but if it's there, they pick up on it. This encourages them to deny responsibility for their misbehavior. It encourages them to argue and point the finger elsewhere.

It's their own form of revenge. It may seem wrong or absurd, or even immature, but it's a normal response when the person enforcing the consequence does so with any level of relish or exasperation. It's a normal response when the teacher lectures, glares, or dresses them down. Oh, the student may very well accept the consequence without complaint, but inside they'll be unrepentant.

If, however, they receive a consequence from someone they like and respect, and it's given impersonally, then the response is quite different. Typically, they'll look down at their feet or stare off into the distance, lost in the thought of their own part in the disruption, transgression, or misbehavior. They'll accept and even agree with your consequence. They'll take responsibility, naturally and without you having to say another word.

When a teacher is well liked, they leave misbehaving students devoid of anything or anyone to blame but themselves. They leave them with eyes clear enough and honest enough to see how their misbehavior affects others. They leave them humbled and determined not to make the same mistake again. It changes them. It flips their attitude from wanting to misbehave behind your back to wanting to please you.

Your steady, day-after-day consistency, in both personality and commitment to accountability, has a transformational effect on students. It proves to them that you walk the walk, that you got their back, that you care enough to protect their right to learn and enjoy school. It proves to them that when you enforce a consequence, it's done purely and from a caring heart. It proves to them that you're a leader worth following.

A Simple Way to Curb Side-Talking

S IDE-TALKING CAN BE ESPECIALLY frustrating because, although it's done out of earshot, it's remarkably disruptive. When your students turn their attention away from you and to a neighbor, they miss important instruction and learning time—which means you'll either have to repeat yourself or reteach individual students after your lesson. It can also delay them from getting their independent work done and distract them from deeper understanding. Furthermore, side-talking begets more side-talking, as students catch the contagion and pass it along to others.

Ignoring the problem just isn't an option. You can certainly enforce a consequence, but an oft-repeated and valid complaint from teachers is that it can be difficult to determine who exactly is doing the side-talking and who is merely listening or asking the other to stop. What follows is a simple, four-step solution. And the best part is, because it's a student-empowered strategy, you don't even have to get involved.

1. Define it.

Before you can begin fixing the problem of side-talking, you must define it for your students. They need to know specifically what your definition of side-talking is and what it looks like. There may be times when you allow it—or a form of it. If so, your students need to know when those times are and what appropriate side-talking looks like. Modeling all forms—right and wrong, appropriate and not—is key to their understanding.

2. Provide them a tool.

Once your students are clear about what side-talking is, and when it is and isn't okay, the next step is to empower them with a tool they can use to curb inappropriate side-talking on their own and without saying a word. The tool you'll show them is a simple hand gesture they'll display to whoever attempts to side-talk with them during a lesson, while immersed in independent work, or whenever you deem unacceptable.

3. Teach them how to use it.

As long as it isn't culturally offensive, any sign or motion of the hand will do. Crossing the first two fingers and shaking lightly is a good way to go. It's a gesture conspicuous enough for you to see from across the room and all students can perform it easily.

To show how it works, sit at a student's desk or in a table group while your class is circled around. Pretend to be focused on your work or a lesson when a classmate leans in to interrupt. Quickly and pleasantly show your signal and then turn back to whatever you were doing.

4. Practice politeness.

It's important to emphasize that the gesture is nothing more than a polite reminder to a friend. It's like saying, *"I'm sorry, but I can't talk right now."* It isn't aggressive or angry and it should never accompany any talking or admonition. Pair students up or put them in groups and have them practice, reminding them to use pleasant facial expressions and body language. Show them precisely and thoroughly how it's done this first time, and they won't do it any other way.

Be sure and also practice the appropriate response when on the receiving end of the gesture. Namely, a quick nod of the head and then back to fulfilling their responsibilities.

When To Enforce

This simple, nonverbal communication between two students attacks the problem at the source and sends the message, each time its given, that interrupting a fellow student during critical listening or independent learning time is off limits. And because it comes from within, it is a powerful deterrent.

It does require a slight addendum to your classroom management plan, but it is a narrow one at that. For if ever your students don't follow the hand-gesture procedure as taught and practiced, or if the gesture is ignored, then a consequence is immediately given. But unlike struggling to figure out who is deserving of a consequence, and getting it wrong much of the time, you'll be able to tell exactly who the culprit is. No arguing, no "it was him, not me," and no wasting time. Just a polite, more focused classroom.

18

How to Stay the Course
With a Tough Class

T HE TOUGHER THE CLASS, the easier it is to be inconsistent. The easier it is to give in and lose control. Which is why when you have a challenging group of students you must be mentally tough. You must be, as Winston Churchill once said, "a peg, hammered into the frozen ground, immovable."

But how? How do you stay the course day after day? How do you stay strong when your students are *trying* to get under your skin? How do you enforce a consequence when it's the last thing in the world you feel like doing? Well, nobody does it naturally. *Everyone* feels resistance. Everyone at times feels a seemingly irresistible pull to cave in, back down, and look the other way.

It can also be difficult to be "on" in every moment. Maybe you're not feeling well. Maybe it's Friday afternoon and you're just *so* ready to call it a day. Maybe things are finally going well and you think, *"Why not just let it go this one time? What's the harm?"* Whatever the reason, failing to follow through on your promises is always a mistake. Which is why you need something you can lean on, an attitude or frame of mind that stays with you and sustains you through your weakest moments.

What follows are three key thoughts that will give you the mental toughness you need to stay the course, no matter how challenging your class.

1. Do it for them.

The most effective teachers have an overabundance of mama/papa bear in them that says, *"It's my job to protect my students' right to learn and enjoy school, and come what may, that's exactly what I'm going to do."* There is no one else to safeguard your students from disruption, bullying, being made fun of, and the like but you. Their school year, their future, and their parent's hopes and dreams for them are at stake. For one year, anyway, they're entirely in your hands. When you embrace this responsibility (and reality), it makes following through and doing right by your students so much easier. In fact, it makes it the most natural thing in the world.

2. Be willing to lose your job.

There is great strength in committing to a task, not merely in a sense that it's something you're determined to do, but rather something you invest in so completely that you allow yourself no other choice. *You will do it.*

A powerful way to embody this feeling is to adopt the attitude that they—administration, powers that be, educational establishment, etc.—will have to fire you and drag you from the classroom to stop you from fulfilling your promises to your students. It represents a level of commitment that will effectively repel all forms of resistance, no matter how strong. Ironically, with this mindset, not only will you never lose your job, but you'll be admired by your colleagues, beloved by your students, and left alone by your principal.

3. Accept that it's the only way.

When your class is out of control and the students seem so disrespectful, callous, and unmotivated, *what you're seeing isn't who they really are.* Poor leadership, ineffective strategies, and inconsistency in the past have created what you're seeing.

The only way to fix it, the only way to sweep away the negativity and reveal the very best in your students—as well as in yourself—is to bring fair, honest, and consistent accountability into the picture. Accepting that it's the only way to peace, the only way to inspired teaching and learning, and the only way to the stress-free career you really want is all the motivation you need to stay the course.

The Way It's Going to Be

Several years ago, there was a rumor that the President was coming by the school I was working at for a visit. (He never did.) Honestly, the first thing that came to my mind was, *"Well, if he comes into my room, he'll have to follow the rules just like everyone else."* I laugh at the thought, but it underscores the level of commitment needed to follow through on your promise to create a safe and enjoyable learning experience for your students. Even if you don't teach in an especially difficult school, or you're not in the midst of trying to turn around an out-of-control class, cultivating a tough mindset is still incredibly valuable. In fact, in time it will become not just an attitude or mentality you carry with you to school every day.

But who you are.

19

One of the Worst Classroom Management Strategies I've Ever Seen

RECENTLY, I HAD A chance to visit a classroom management training for new teachers. The trainer was an expert in a program that has gained popularity in recent years. I won't mention the program by name, but at its core, it's a token economy, whereby students are rewarded in exchange for "good" (i.e. expected) behavior.

I've written about this strategy before. If you've been a reader of SCM long enough, then you know how strongly we feel about token economies. They send the message that expected behavior—that which is minimally required for success in school—is worthy of special recognition, turning what is inherently rewarding into *work* students deserve to be paid for.

They also encourage unethical behavior like cheating and stealing. They weaken the student-teacher relationship, making it coldhearted, transactional, and even hurtful. They make creating a happy and productive classroom harder, not easier. Worst of all, though, token economies snuff out intrinsic motivation.

But on this day, as I stood in the back of the room, the trainer was demonstrating how to handle misbehaving students using a form of praise called "caught being good." The way it works is that if you notice a student misbehaving and off task, instead of holding them accountable using a predetermined set of rules and consequences, you would praise the students around them. In other words, you would ignore the misbehaving student, but effusively inform those in proximity how wonderful they are for doing *what they're supposed to do.*

The idea, in theory, is that the student in question would also want to receive praise, and thus would be compelled to stop their unwanted behavior. So what's the problem? Well, besides being dishonest, it communicates that fulfilling the barest minimum is somehow special and on par with what is truly exceptional—lowering the bar of excellence down around the shoe tops.

It's also cruel and demeaning and, in this case, uses well-behaved students as pawns to elicit compliant behavior from the misbehaving student. Furthermore, it offers no genuine feedback they can use to improve their behavior in the future.

That this method is endorsed, taught, and even promoted in school districts around the country is tragic and shameful. It takes the high calling of being a teacher and tosses it into the gutter of trickery and manipulation, ripping apart both its heart and its soul.

Teaching isn't about just getting through the day. It isn't about curbing misbehavior momentarily or deceiving students into doing what you want. It's about inspiring real change in students and making an impact that lasts a lifetime.

So what's the alternative? Be straight with your students. Establish a boundary line of behavior that protects their right to learn and enjoy school and then defend it to the hilt. Do what you say you're going to do. Hold them accountable fairly and respectfully and give them the opportunity to learn from their mistakes.

Praise only what is praiseworthy. Look for legitimate improvement, new learning, or greater effort than they've given before, and then let them know you notice. Smile and make eye contact from across the room. Leave a note folded over and attached to their desk. Tell them they did well. Shine a light on concrete evidence of their progress.

Treat every student with dignity, eschewing all forms of false praise, bribery, and disingenuousness—which only set them up for future failure and disappointment. Be the same dependable, consistent teacher every day. Build relationships based on love and forgiveness, kindness and honesty, humor and humility.

Look your students in the eye and tell them the truth about their successes and mistakes, as well as their failures and triumphs. *Give them feedback they can use.* Prepare them for life beyond the classroom by being a leader worthy of their respect and admiration. This way, your words of praise will mean something to them, firing their intrinsic motivational engines deep within their heart. They'll know that if you said it, it must be true. And the truth will set them free.

20

How to Eliminate Cell Phone Use From the Classroom

THIS PAST WEEK, I watched the first episode of A&E's Undercover High. To the uninitiated, the show follows seven young adults who go undercover in an American high school. One of the things that struck me, among many, was the ubiquity of cell phone use *in class*. Cameras showed teachers trying to give instruction while students checked social media, texted, and listened to music. I felt bad for the teachers, but even more so for the students. Here they were in the midst of perhaps their best opportunity to begin creating a life of meaning and contribution, and it was passing them by.

Sadly, the use of cell phones during instructional time is a pervasive problem that is only growing in intensity—and not just in high school. In the past year, I've been inundated with emails from teachers of students as young as sixth grade who are at their wit's end.

In this particular episode, it became evident that the school's policy on cell phones in the classroom was that students shouldn't use them. Which, of course, means absolutely nothing. It puts teachers in the position of merely discouraging their use, which in this day and age is a near impossible task. Unless your content and ability to deliver it are more compelling than the highly addictive nature of cell phones, then learning will be profoundly and negatively affected.

So what's the solution? Well, the first step is to create a school-wide policy that bans cell phones from *even being pulled out in class*, whether from a backpack, purse, or pocket. Merely banning their use doesn't go far enough and will only lead to arguing and battling with students over what, exactly, this means. The policy must be clear-cut, easy to define, and easy to determine whether it's been broken. Thus, if a phone is exposed to the light of day—no matter the circumstance—then the policy has been broken. In this way, it either is or isn't. There is no gray area or possibility open to interpretation.

As for consequences, I recommend that phones be taken away without students first receiving a warning. Otherwise, they'll use up their warning every chance they get. An immediate consequence also sends the message that learning is sacred and anything that interferes with it is a serious offense.

But you can't just one day begin demanding that students hand over their most cherished possession. They must first understand the policy in full. They must know why it's in place as well as how their phone will be taken away and when and how it will be returned. Laying the policy out clearly and completely beforehand, so there are no misunderstandings or opportunities to shift the blame elsewhere, goes a long way toward avoiding defiance, disrespect, and refusal to give up their phone when the policy is enforced. Therefore, it's essential to hold a school-wide assembly explaining your policy in detail.

As for specifics, I recommend the following:

- If a student pulls out their phone at any time between the start and end of class—determined by the bell schedule or crossing the threshold into a classroom—then the student loses their phone for the rest of the day. It doesn't matter if they put their phone away before the teacher approaches or if they pull it out for a quick second to check the time. If it comes out, regardless of why, the policy has been broken. *Note:* This also includes the use of headphones. In other words, if a student has headphones (or earbuds) out and visible, whether they're listening to them or not, it's the same as having their phone out. Both the headphones and phone, then, would be taken away.

- The teacher takes possession of the phone by approaching the student and holding open a large ziplock bag. By using a plastic bag rather than taking the phone by hand, it shows respect for the student's property. It's also less confrontational and causes students to be more comfortable handing it over. This also underscores the importance of not lecturing, scolding, or making a show of taking the phone. The teacher then secures the bag and immediately places it in a drawer or cabinet that can be locked for safekeeping.

- At the end of the day, the student must return to class to retrieve their phone. You may include in the policy that if the student doesn't arrive a certain time, then they must wait until the following morning. It isn't the teacher who must be inconvenienced.

- If a student is a repeat offender, defined by breaking the policy a second time during a grading period (semester or quarter), then the phone must be retrieved *by a parent* before or after school in the main office. In this case, the teacher would label the bag and turn the phone over to designated office personnel as soon as they're able. At this point it's important that administration gets involved by issuing further consequence. A detention and lowering of citizenship grade (if applicable) for each time the policy is broken after the first incident will strengthen the policy and lessen the chances of it happening again.

- If a student chooses not to give up their phone, then there must be an immediate referral to administration, lowering of citizenship grade, and escalation to a stronger consequence. This may include a week of lunch detention, after-school cleanup, Saturday school, or other.

- The only exception to any of the above is if the teacher authorizes the use of a phone for a specific, sharply defined educational purpose within a set time limit.

And that's it. It's clear. It's simple and straightforward. It's easy to understand and easy to implement. Most important, however, it's proven effective. But here's the thing: Everyone must buy in. Every teacher and administrator on campus must follow the policy as it's written in the student handbook. Otherwise, it isn't worth the paper it's printed on. Students will soon discover that you don't really mean what you say, and you'll be right back where you started.

If you stick with it, however, and refrain from offering friendly reminders and warnings or pretending you didn't see what you just saw, not only will you eliminate this one highly addictive distraction, but all forms of misbehavior will improve. It will raise the level of respect and responsibility in your entire school.

It's important to note that if you're an individual teacher who works at a school that has turned a blind eye to the problem, perhaps they have a policy but don't follow it or it's similar to the Undercover High policy, then theoretically you can create your own policy. You can also fold it into the classroom management plan we recommend for high school teachers. However, although it's possible, it takes a teacher with a strong set of relationship and classroom management skills—of the kind we teach at SCM— to make it effective. Otherwise, it could be more trouble than it's worth.

A better solution is to band together as a staff. Start a conversation with your closest colleagues. Schedule a meeting with the principal. Put it on the agenda of the next staff meeting. Introduce the policy above and put it to a vote. Change happens when tough, smart people decide to speak up and take a stand for those who can't—namely, the scores of students whose chance for a quality education is being undermined and trampled underfoot by this one insidious habit.

One last thing. If you think that at your school the problem is too big to fix, I just have one word for you: Hogwash. It will work *anywhere* and at any school that commits to it and decides that enough is enough. Every student deserves an opportunity to learn without distraction.

So what are you waiting for?

PART THREE:
Influence

21

The Best Incentive You Could Ever Give

BECAUSE I BELIEVE IT'S a mistake to reward students for good behavior, I'm often asked, "So, then, the stickers, prizes, and such . . . should teachers refrain from giving them out at all?" Well, yes and no. Anything that whiffs of bribery should be avoided. No doubt about it. Promising a reward if your students do this or that—or don't do this or that—creates a Pandora's box of new problems and doesn't change behavior in the long run. Simply by cutting incentives of this nature out of your program, will not only calm and mature your students, and begin fueling their intrinsic motivation, but it will make your teaching life gloriously easier.

This doesn't mean, however, that you have to throw away your prize box or stop giving out pencils and stickers altogether. In fact, when presented in a certain way, they can indeed help improve behavior—albeit in an indirect but much more authentic way.

The key is in the giving.

Instead of doling out prizes based on what you receive in return (i.e. good behavior), you'll hand them out for no reason at all. In other words, they become no longer an incentive in the traditional sense, but a free gift. *"Hey, before you leave for the day, I've got cool pencils for everyone!"*

It's a simple way of showing your love and appreciation for your class. Nothing more. But here's the thing. Small gestures like this, along with the personality you bring with you to the classroom, will cause your class to reciprocate that love. And herein lies its power. Creating a classroom your students look forward to is the most powerful incentive you could ever offer—bar none. It is so effective, in fact, that the leverage and influence it affords you is the key to having the rewarding teaching experience you've always longed for.

It's important to note that you don't *have* to give out pencils or prizes, or anything at all. It isn't required. But if it's something you enjoy doing, then it can certainly add another element of fun and enjoyment to your classroom.

A common complaint from teachers is that they're under-appreciated by students. But this is a natural consequence of using rewards in exchange for good behavior. To students, it's a tit-for-tat business transaction. And it takes the heart and soul right out of the relationship. *I do this, you give that, and we're even.*

I know a particularly effective third grade teacher who on Friday afternoons holds what she calls a dance party. Ten minutes before dismissal she puts on some music and her students get up and go for it—the wildest and silliest dances you've ever seen. They love it and look forward to it every week. The dance party isn't a reward, however, and it isn't a strategy. It's nothing more than an expression of joy, an uninhibited celebration of another week of learning together. It's also one more reason to love being in her class.

Now, a very interesting happens while the students are dancing. The teacher will walk around the room pretending to be a judge. She'll pull glasses down on her face, carry a clipboard, and make believe she's scribbling notes. Every once in a while she'll point to a student, or a group dancing together, and say, "Go get something from the prize box!" They'll rush over and pick out a bouncy ball or bracelet and then rejoin the party.

She chooses different students every week, and they all get chosen multiple times, but you may be wondering, *"Don't the other students get upset when they're not picked to get a prize?"*

The answer is no, because they know that a trip to the prize box or a rare sticker or pencil giveaway is an entirely free gift. It can't be earned. There is no heartless exchange of goods and services. There is no bribery or manipulation. There is no "do this and get that" culture to produce envy and jealousy. There is just a classroom they can't wait to get to every day. And this makes all the difference.

22

The Easiest Way to Improve
Classroom Behavior

THE EASIEST WAY TO improve classroom behavior is one few teachers ever consider. It's at once blatantly obvious and far off the grid. You won't find it in modern professional books and are unlikely to hear about it at conferences. Yet, it's as plain as day and works every time.

It doesn't entail making drastic changes. It doesn't entail extra planning or specialized training. It doesn't entail selling, persuading, or convincing your students of anything. In fact, they'll be all for it. For it is both a universal truth and a welcome balm to any human interaction.

So what is this miracle strategy? It's politeness. Walk into any polite classroom anywhere in the world and there you will find well-behaved students. You'll find happiness and harmony, smiles and friendship, community and contentment.

So how do you bring more politeness into your classroom? You teach it. You model what it looks like. You practice and encourage it until it becomes part of the fabric of your classroom. Teachers who focus on this one oft-neglected strategy have far fewer problems with classroom management. They have fewer problems with disrespect, bullying, bickering, and the like.

If you've never taught politeness before, the most effective approach is to focus on just three foundational areas.

1. Please and thank you.
2. Hello and goodbye.
3. Excuse me and after you.

These three alone will change the tone of your classroom, inspire more profound acts of kindness, and result in better overall classroom behavior.

The first step in teaching them is to model what they look like. Ask for volunteers to help you as you act out how to greet a classmate, how to accept a helping hand, or how to pause and allow someone to pass in front of you. Use everyday examples from the classroom while emphasizing the importance of tone, body language, and eye contact. Once you've covered each foundational area, break your students into groups and let them practice on their own. Pose common situations and then give them a few minutes to role-play each one.

A tablemate is leaving for the day.
Two students approach the tissue box at the same time.
A classmate helps you on an assignment.
You accidentally bump into someone while lining up for lunch.

Periodic refreshers throughout the year are a good idea, but gentle reminders keep it going. Good teachers are in the habit of stage-whispering cues whenever a student forgets.

"Please."
"Good morning."
"Excuse me."

These simple words, conveyed with a smile just a few times a week, will sustain and nurture the kind, considerate, and well-behaved learning environment you're after. But you must be the leader, the chief role model, the pillar of politeness. Every day. Sarcasm, impatience, and grouchiness will undo any good vibrations you've created.

Teaching politeness is a simple little thing. Easily disregarded, quickly forgotten, and too 1950s for today's educational complexities. But in the hands of a teacher willing to make it a priority, it's powerful stuff. It transforms and uplifts. It endures and inspires. It leaves a mark that never fades away.

23

Why Good Rapport With Students Is a Choice You Make Every Day

T HE IMPORTANCE OF HAVING good rapport with students can't be overstated. Because rapport gives you leverage. It gives you leadership presence and the influence to *change* behavior. It causes students to *want* to listen, learn, and behave for you, even when they're hellions with other teachers. It's also the ingredient that makes teaching one of the most rewarding professions on Earth.

Building rapport is easier than most teachers realize. It doesn't take any extra time or effort. You don't have to spend your prep hour chatting with students or playing foursquare—although there is nothing wrong with doing so. You don't have to have the gift of small talk or a comedian's wit. You don't have to be anyone but yourself.

But it does take a choice. You see, in any leadership position there is a risk for developing negative thoughts about those given into your care, especially if you're struggling with rebellious or unruly behavior. And this can be very, very dangerous. Because when you dislike or resent any one or more of your students, *they'll know it*. It's something you can't hide. Your negative feelings about them will bubble to the surface one way or another. They'll come out in your body language, facial expressions, and tone of voice. They'll come out in the words you use and the vibe you give off.

Have you ever heard the expression, 'Your thoughts are showing?' It's a truism that becomes heightened in any position of leadership, whether teacher, coach, or parent. Children in particular are ultra sensitive to how adults perceive them.

So, while the key to building influential rapport is nothing more than being consistently pleasant, it's only possible if you choose to like your students. And it's very much a choice. It isn't a reaction, a feeling, an intuition, or a hope. It isn't based on how they look, how studious they are, or whether or not they're outwardly friendly. It doesn't even matter if they're disrespectful, misbehave behind your back, or try to ruin your best lessons. You choose to like them anyway.

And here's the amazing thing: Once you commit yourself to like every student and see only the best in them—no matter who they are or what they've done in the past—they become not so unlikable after all. Because when you choose to like them, consciously and relentlessly, they begin to like you right back, even the most difficult among them.

They begin to behave differently around you, smiling and making eye contact. They begin to trust you and want to please you. They become different people altogether. It's a virtuous cycle that only gets stronger with time.

So, practically, on the first day of school and thereafter, make it a point to smile at every student. Talk to them like you would your best and most well-behaved students. And keep at it day after day. *Choose* to be happy to see them.

Yes, some days it may take a few quiet moments alone before school to remind yourself that you're going to doggedly like

Anthony or Karla or whoever despite how they behaved the day before. But you do it because it has a direct and profound effect on your ability to motivate, inspire, and be the teacher your students need and respond best to. You do it because it brings peace and joy to your classroom. You do it because it's the right thing to do.

Building influential rapport isn't difficult. It's available to any teacher who guards their heart and mind against negativity, animosity, and resentment. It's a choice, not a skill. It's a choice that can mean the difference between success and failure. Hope and disillusionment. Love and hate.

What Building Relationships
With Students Really Means

I T'S COMMON FOR TEACHERS to misunderstand the term "building relationships." They hear of the importance of creating connections with students—particularly difficult students—and assume it means they need to spend more time with them individually. They assume it means they need to try and get to know them on a more personal level.

But for a real-world teacher, finding the time to build relationships in this manner is not only unrealistic, but it's also ineffective. In fact, seeking out individual students in an attempt to earn their trust and rapport can do more harm than good. You see, for most students, being cornered into a non-academic conversation with their teacher is uncomfortable—exceedingly so. It can make them feel clumsy and self-conscious and at a loss of anything to say. Even the most socially confident students will feel unnerved and wary of your motives. And yet, there are teachers who insist on pressing the issue day after day.

They beckon students out of line, into hallways, and away from the social safety of fellow classmates. They barge into their personal space. They query their likes and dislikes and commonalities. They become forward and overbearing.

Although their heart is in the right place, what develops is a relationship of awkwardness and embarrassment. What develops is defensiveness and detachment. What develops builds walls instead of tearing them down.

The goal of building relationships with students isn't familiarity. It's influence. And influence comes about not by one-on-one interactions, not by getting to know a student's favorite ice cream or video game, and not by being hip to current pop-cultural trends. No, influential relationships come about through your trustworthiness and likability.

If your students trust you because you always do what you say will, and they like you because you're consistently pleasant, then powerful, behavior-influencing rapport will happen naturally and without you having to work at it. Your students will seek *you* out and want to be around you and get to know you better. They'll be drawn to you and pulled effortlessly into your circle of influence.

Your conversations and interactions then become open and easy. When you sit down to lunch with *groups* of students or meet them in their line before school, the give-and-take flows smoothly, organically. Nothing is forced. Nothing is inauthentic. Even quiet and shy students—especially quiet and shy students—will come out of the woodwork to laugh and joke with you and exchange goofy smiles. This in turn gives you remarkable leverage to influence behavior, work habits, and enthusiasm for being part of your classroom.

So stop buying into the notion that you have to build relationships one student at a time. Stop thinking that you have to add yet another time-consuming strategy to your overflowing plate. Stop spending more time with some students and not others.

The fact is, the most effective way to build relationships with students also happens to be the most effective approach to classroom management.

Be true to your word. Follow through with your classroom management plan. Refrain from any and all harmful, scolding, bribing, manipulative, or friction-creating methods of managing behavior. Smile. Love your students. Bring humor and joy to your classroom. And you'll never, ever have to *try* to build influential relationships again. They'll just happen.

9 Ways to Have More Authority

AUTHORITY PLAYS AN IMPORTANT role in effective classroom management because it affects how students view you. It affects how well they listen to you and follow your directions. It affects their behavior around you, their trust in you, and their respect for you.

Some teachers seem to have it right out of the box. They walk into a room and students immediately sense a strong, sure leadership presence. And it changes them. They become calmer, more mature, and more polite. It imbues them with a desire to please and behave and be better students and people.

Although, at first glance, authority appears to be an inborn gift reserved for a lucky few, there is really no mystery at all. Anyone can have more of it by emulating the following nine traits.

1. Dress neatly.
Teachers are dressing more casually now than ever before. You'll do well to buck the trend, because it has an effect on whether students perceive you as a leader worth following. This doesn't mean that you must dress formally or wear expensive clothes. General neatness in appearance and quality of clothing is key.

Dress like the leader you are and your students will treat you with greater respect. Sharp clothing will also make you feel more confident, which will further improve your authority.

2. Stand tall.

Confidence in the way you carry yourself sends the message to students that you know what's best for them and that you're steering them in the right direction. This frees them to let their guard down, accept your words as true, and place their trust in you.

So stand tall. Throw your shoulders back. Move, behave, and express yourself as if you know exactly what you're doing. If you're not *feeling* confident, that's okay. The appearance of confidence can have the same effect. According to research, simply changing your posture can make you feel more powerful and thus behave more confidently.

3. Follow through.

This one is huge. Do what you say you're going to do and over time your authority will skyrocket. Be wishy-washy, however, break your promises and ignore your classroom management plan, and you'll lose authority quickly. Everything you say will be called into question. Your students will challenge you, argue with you, or pay you little mind. Some may even try to take control of the classroom right out of your hands.

4. Honor the truth.

Be upfront and honest in all your dealings with students. Refuse to engage in over-the-top flattery or manipulation. Steer clear of do-this and get-that rewards, catching students doing good, or token economies—which effectively snuff out intrinsic motivation.

Make your words of praise genuine and based on true accomplishment. Tell your students the truth about where they are both behaviorally and academically.

A direct approach is highly motivational. It will give you strong authority as well as dignity and morality that are common to all great leaders.

5. Be Pleasant.

The use of intimidation in any form is terrible leadership. Lecturing, glaring, scolding, and losing your cool may frighten students into behaving in the short term, but the price is your respect, plummeting authority, and more and more misbehavior.

Being consistently pleasant, on the other hand, will give you effortless rapport, powerful leverage, and behavior-changing influence. It will cause students to like you and want to get to know you better, without any additional effort from you. It will make your classroom management plan *matter* to them and work like it should.

6. Be calm.

Teachers who rush around, who are frazzled, scatter-brained, and tense, will never have the same level of authority as those who are calm and prepared. It's not even close. Nervous energy has a way of spreading throughout the classroom, infecting every inch. It causes excitability, inattentiveness, and a form of misbehavior that is very difficult to eliminate. It also makes you look like you don't know what you're doing.

7. Improve your speaking.

Teachers who struggle to gain authority tend to talk fast and ramble on and on. They repeat themselves and fill silences with ums and ers. They include details and asides that neither help nor advance learning. They *over* communicate.

To improve your authority, as well as learning and interest, slow down. Be concise and stay on message. Finish your sentences and pause often to give your class a chance to comprehend what you say. This will cause students to lean in and focus. It will draw them *to* you rather than push them away

8. Be physically prepared.

You can't be an effective teacher, or one your students look up to, if you're stressed out, tired, and irritable. Good teaching requires you to be at your best every day of the week. Which means you must become efficient with lesson planning. You must stay focused during work hours and learn to say no. You must be productive rather than just busy.

Go home at a decent hour and get away from even thinking about school for a few hours. Get your rest, exercise for energy, and sit down to eat real, whole food. Spend time with your family and friends or enjoy your favorite hobby. This will not only improve your authority and likability, but it will also make you a calmer, happier teacher.

9. Choose to see only the best.

Negative thoughts—about students, your job, the curriculum, etc.—have a way of bubbling to the surface and revealing themselves in your behavior, body language, facial expressions, and even in the things that you say. It's something you can't hide. And it will severely damage your ability to be an effective teacher.

Great teaching and inspired leadership is predicated on setting aside negative self-talk, refusing to engage in it and choosing instead to see only the best in the people, situations, and circumstances at hand.

It's a choice, after all. It's a choice that has a profound effect on how your students view you—as well as on your very happiness.

Do You Have It?

The nine ways to improve authority will separate you from the pack. They'll cause students to decide within just a few minutes of sizing you up that you're someone worth their attention and respect. They may not be able to put their finger on what it is about you that is special. But they'll know it's there, and that it's different and powerful. You just have it.

You have that secret something, that inexplicable mystery of presence and authority that causes parents and staff members alike to whisper words like charismatic, gifted, and "a natural" when describing you. But the truth is, it's nothing more than a set of traits available to anyone. They're available to anyone willing to adopt them for themselves and dare to be more than just another teacher.

26

How to Bring Instant Calm to Your Classroom

O NE OF THE BIGGEST causes of misbehavior is excitability. It's also one of the hardest to fix. The reason is that most struggling teachers just don't notice it. They become so used to the tension, so accustomed to the antsiness and disquiet, that they're not even aware it exists. A visitor, however, can feel it the moment they step through the door. It's palpable. Personally, the buzz of excitability gives me the heebie-jeebies. It makes me shiver and takes willpower just to stick around for a few minutes.

The good news is that once it's identified, once it's determined to be the root cause of silliness, rambunctiousness, and the like, it can be corrected almost instantly with the following five strategies.

1. Breathe.

You are the source of the energy in your classroom. Your students take up their cue from *you*. So if you're tense and uptight, it will reflect in the behavior of your class.

One sure way to sweep out the negative vibes is to breathe, long and slow, deep through the abdomen. Relax your body and let your calm presence fill the room and carry from one student to the next. I know it sounds new-agey, but it really works. You can feel the pressure drain from your room and actually see restlessness and excitability subside. Just breathe and soften the muscles of your body. Not only will it have a positive effect on your students, but it will help alleviate your own mental stress and strain.

2. Pause.

Struggling teachers tend to talk fast with very little space between phrases. They also pepper their speech with ums and ahs, fearing that if they don't fill the silence, then their students will. Add to it the overwhelming need to narrate and over-explain and repeat themselves again and again, and you have the perfect recipe for excitability.

You see, the constant chatter is disconcerting to students. It causes nervousness and boredom and the desire to tune you out in favor of those around them. Simply pausing—often and sometimes lengthily—increases the power of your words. It makes you more interesting. It saves students the bandwidth they need to fully take in what you have to say. It stops the turning and racing of their thoughts and enables them to settle in and just listen.

3. Stop.

Watching a teacher move and bustle around the room all day is both exhausting and nerve-wracking to students. Many teachers think it causes them to pay better attention. But the opposite is true. It causes them to grow weary, lose focus, and look away. The solution is to stop and stand in one place, especially when giving instructions or providing important information. This will draw eyes and ears *to* you. It will pull your students' attention away from every little distraction in the environment and focus it on what matters.

4. Reduce.

Most teachers talk too much and struggling teachers talk *way* too much. The result is that within a short period of time, ten minutes even, the flood of information becomes overwhelming to students. They can only take in so much. They can only pick out and decipher what's important for so long before they completely tune you out. Your voice then becomes background noise that merely agitates and inspires their own chatter. If you can cut your talking by one third, you'll notice a dramatic difference in attentiveness. Your students will have time to process, ponder, and comprehend. And they'll come to know that everything you say is worth listening to.

5. Slow.

Excitability is like listening to a song played at twice the speed. It's like running errands on one too many cups of coffee or watching a sugar high romp in a birthday party bounce house. A sure way to quell an overstimulated class is to simply slow down. Talk slower. Move slower. Take your time between transitions. Never move on until you're getting exactly what you want from your students.

Remarkably, you'll find that not only will your class be calmer and more focused, but you'll get *a lot* more done. Listening and performance will also improve, and you'll have more time than you ever thought possible.

Bad Juju

Excitability is an oft-hidden but potent cause of misbehavior. It's an ever-present hum that once taken hold, never leaves your classroom. Unless, that is, you recognize it for the scourge that it is and deal with it at its source. The five strategies above are proven to calm and soothe even the most frazzled classrooms. They rid the air of bad juju. They settle unsettled minds. They eliminate the desire to fidget and squirm and talk a mile a minute.

But they must become not merely strategies you try once in a while or when things get particularly chaotic. Rather, they must become as much a part of your classroom as the desks and chairs and the curriculum you so badly want to be able to teach.

27

Why Service is a Powerful Classroom Management Strategy

NCOURAGING YOUR STUDENTS TO become service-oriented is a powerful classroom management strategy. Because it creates empathy. It causes them to see their classmates as people just like them, with the same hopes, feelings, and struggles. It virtually eliminates bullying and improves self-worth. Most importantly, it opens their eyes to how disruptive behavior, particularly their own, affects those around them—which very effectively improves that behavior. Focusing on service also teaches life lessons, brings disparate students together in friendship, and improves cooperation and teamwork.

But the big question is how? How do you become a classroom that is altruistic and unselfish in nature? What follows are three simple things you can do to encourage service beginning the first day of school.

1. Define what service is.

Before your students can begin looking outside of themselves in the service of others, they need to know what it is. To that end, I recommend teaching the following definition:

1. Service is an active form of helpfulness. Meaning, you don't wait until someone asks.
2. It's something you look for and act upon, even when it's inconvenient.
3. Most often, it's as simple as listening, smiling, or just being a friend.

You may also want to cover specific examples, such as how to welcome a new student or how to recognize if someone is struggling or feeling down—as well as how to approach them and what to say.

2. Model it with your behavior.

Your students are more influenced by what you do than what you say. Therefore, your own acts of kindness and service—greeting students, smiling, asking how they are, looking them in the eye and listening, even reaching down and picking up a dropped pencil—can have a powerful effect. These simple, humble gestures have a way of rubbing off on students, multiplying and bouncing from one to the next throughout your room like a happy game of telephone. This helps ensure that no student feels left behind, lost in the cracks, or shoved into the margins of school culture—as so many do and are.

3. Go out and do it.

As I wrote in *Dream Class*, serving others outside of your classroom and into the wider school community has a calming effect. It develops open-mindedness, maturity, and selflessness. It gets students out of their heads, turning their attention away from their own wants and desires and into a healthier direction. And the amazing thing is, it's instantaneous.

The moment you return to class from cleaning up the auditorium or raking the garden or helping out in a special education classroom, you'll notice greater peace and contentment in your students. At first, a small number may complain or feel uncomfortable, but the more you do it—even in small doses—the more agreeable they become and the more effective it is.

It Feels Good

One wonderful thing about this strategy is that you don't have to work hard at it. I've found that service is something today's students in particular are quick to latch onto. It seems to come more naturally to this generation than those of the past.

As for finding the time for it, with good classroom management comes the freedom not to have to rush through *anything*. It buys you oceans of time few other teachers enjoy. I've also found that even in this day of strict schedules and timetables, as long as you speak to your principal ahead of time, explain why you want to help out in a lower-grade classroom, for example, or beautify the joint-use park, they're usually enthusiastically supportive.

So I encourage you. Make your classroom more than just the acquisition of knowledge. Develop the whole person by being a classroom defined by service. It feels good. It has wonderful mental benefits for both the doer and the receiver. And improves behavior while you're at it.

28

Why Caring Too Much Can Make You a Less Effective Teacher

TEACHING IS IMPORTANT, TO be sure. But if you're not careful, this fact can weigh heavily. It can cause you to wrap an unhealthy amount of your identity into your job. It can cause you to be distracted around your friends and family. It can cause you to care *too much*.

And when you care too much, not only are you wrung out, preoccupied, and no fun to be around, but you make mistakes that make you a less effective teacher. You become personally offended when students misbehave. You become irritable, easily frustrated, and less approachable. You become so invested in your students' success, so pressured by administrative powers, that you begin doing for them what only they can do for themselves.

The truth is, the most effective teachers maintain a level of professional distance—from their students, their classroom, and even their school. They view teaching as a two-way street. Meaning, they give their best for their students. They teach high-interest lessons. They build leverage and influence through their consistent pleasantness and likability. They create a learning experience their students *want* to be a part of.

But they also expect the best in return, which manifests itself in everything they do. From enforcing consequences dispassionately to giving directions one time to their reluctance to kneel down and reteach individuals what was taught to the entire class minutes before, their actions announce to the world their deep and abiding belief in their students.

You see, when you take on what are your students' responsibilities, even emotionally, they'll be left with the message that they have a free pass. So they shrug in response to your urgent exhortations. They ignore your requests for quiet. They listen only when convenient. They daydream and side-talk and count tiles on the ceiling. It never occurs to them that they're sitting in a sacred place of learning or that they desperately need what you have to offer. The result is a stressed out teacher and a class full of students who just don't care.

In the most effective classrooms, responsibilities are clearly separate and defined. The teacher does their job well, providing everything their students need to be successful, then hands the onus to do the work, discuss the book, perform the experiment, and solve for x in full over to their students.

Your job is to teach, inspire, and hold accountable—which is completely in your control. When you focus your physical and emotional energy on these three core responsibilities, and you are determined to turn the rest over to your students, your stress will all but disappear. At the same time, the whole vibe of your classroom will change. The winds of complacency and apathy will die out. Balance will be restored to the kingdom.

Your students will feel the burden of responsibility for learning and behaving settle upon their shoulders, where it belongs. Their respect for you will soar. Their sense of independence will swell. Rapport will come easy—light and effortless.

Your heavy mood, your hurt, and your disappointment will lift and dissipate into the heavens. You'll have the energy you need to create your dream class. And you'll finally be able to leave school at school.

Now both you and your students will possess the same look: Happy yet determined. Calm yet filled with purpose. Fulfilled yet resolute.

The way it's supposed to be.

When and Why It's Okay
for Students to Talk

THERE IS A COMMON misconception that effective classroom management means silence. It means rigidness and
tight restriction. It means backs straight and eyes forward,
hour after hour. And while there are teachers who try to run their
classroom this way, or think they should, at SCM we think it's
a terrible idea because it limits social and academic growth. It
causes boredom, resentment, and a strong dislike for school. It
makes every day an agonizing, tension-filled slog to dismissal.

Of course, there are blocks of time throughout the day when
your students should be quiet. Uninterrupted independent work, to
use one example, is a critical component of learning. But this is an
academic strategy, not a way to keep students under your thumb.

To create a healthy, well-behaved environment, your students
need breaks. They need opportunities to stretch their legs and
recharge their batteries. Teacher-led exercises are a good idea.
Jumping jacks, desk push-ups, air curls, arm circles, static poses,
and jogging-in-place are simple ways to clear the boards and
provide energy for the next activity. Dancing and lip syncing
to music, depending on your grade level, also work well and are

especially fun. Just a few minutes between lessons add flavor to the day and give students another reason to love school.

But there is one particular type of break that seems to work best of all. It's fast and easy and students really, *really* appreciate it. It's talking.

Now, it's important to point out that letting students *continue to talk* because that's what they're already doing is a bad idea and will only make matters worse. The form of talking I'm referring to is structured and defined by the teacher. In other words, you first model what a talking break looks like before letting your students loose. You lay out your expectations by showing precisely what is and isn't okay. A reminder that you'll follow your classroom management plan as usual is also a good idea.

I recommend giving your students two to four minutes to move about the room and talk with whomever they wish. As for the topic, you can either let them chat about whatever they like or, again, depending on your grade level, provide a topic for them. *"Share with someone your favorite superhero and why."*

Bookend the break with a signal to start and a signal to return to their seats. I like to begin abruptly with something like "Get up and say hello to your friends!" and close with simply "Times up." When it's over and you're ready to move on to the next lesson or activity, you'll have a more receptive class. They'll sit up a little straighter and listen more intently. They'll have more energy to focus and the clarity of mind to better understand.

Giving students a few minutes to talk with their friends is a simple little thing. But it effectively shakes the restlessness out of their system. It wakes them up and gets the blood flowing. It activates the brain and buoys the heart. It settles, it calms, it motivates. It prepares them for the challenges that lie ahead.

30

How Read-Aloud Can Improve Behavior and Instill a Lifelong Love of Reading

I LOVE TO READ ALOUD. I find it to be one of the great joys of teaching. Done in a certain way, it's also an effective classroom management strategy. It encourages a more respectful, peaceful room environment. It calms, soothes, and inspires. It generates *interest* in the things of school and learning. Through wonder, laughter, tears, and adventure, it sets imaginations afire.

Sadly, in recent years, much of the joy of read-aloud has been sucked out and driven away by over-instruction.

"What's the topic sentence?"
"What can you infer from the setting?"
"What evidence supports your conclusion?"
"Can you predict what's going to happen next?"
"What questions do you have for the main character?"
"What do you think they're thinking and why?
"Write down your connections and annotations on a sticky note."
"Turn and tell a partner what you would do in a similar situation."

All while we butcher up the heart and soul of great stories. We undermine their drama, their excitement and tension, their humor, sadness, uncertainty, and raw emotion. We turn works of art into just another academic exercise, destroying the very qualities that draw students into a love of reading. The truth is, if we just focus on being good stewards and deliverers of the material *as it was meant to be consumed*, then all the skills we try to force upon our students happen naturally and far more effectively.

At the same time, we make our classroom a place that embraces the pure joy of reading—*which is far and away the most important point*. We cause our students to want to listen and know and be curious about the world. That look on their faces when they're completely consumed, goners, lost in the story? It bleeds into every other academic subject and area of classroom management. Why would we ever interfere with that?

What follows are four ways to ensure that your read-aloud is a force for all things good and holy rather than the drudgery it has become.

1. Don't stop.

Once you begin a read-aloud, don't stop until you run out of time. Don't stop to analyze the text, explain vocabulary, ask questions, or take breaks for students to discuss. Instead, allow them to get lured in by the story itself. Let them picture the mood, scene, setting, and characters through their own fresh imagination. Let them transport down into another world as you paint the picture.

2. Don't teach.

If teaching how good readers naturally think is something you're required to do, then keep these lessons separate from read-aloud. Break down a paragraph from an unrelated excerpt, short story, or non-fiction text and leave the great books and poems alone—at least until after you've finished them. Honor the story and author and read them from start to finish and as they were intended. Let the narrative progress and grow in the minds of your students pure and untainted.

3. Don't make them sit.

Although read-aloud can improve everything from writing to listening to behavior to class unity, the core purpose is to instill a love of reading (and school). To further deepen this purpose, instead of asking students to sit at their desks or cross-legged on individual squares, allow them to sit or lay about however or wherever they choose. As long as you can see them, let them listen, dream, and imagine in whatever way that suits them.

4. Don't make them share.

Although there is nothing wrong with allowing students to share their thoughts if they wish after each day's reading, make it unprompted, voluntary, and informal.

Give them a break from the pair-shares, writing responses, and the like. And for gosh sakes, don't put any of the text up on your SMART board and start marking it up. Just let the twists and turns, the drama and revelations linger in their minds as they go about their day.

5. Don't skip.

Being able to read aloud and share your own love of books is one of the best things about teaching. So embrace it. *Become* each character. Use voices, inflection, and movement to add depth and richness to the story.

But do stick to the story. In fact, read every word of it. The author spent many months, even years, choosing the perfect dialogue, descriptions, and rhythm in order to make the greatest impact. So let the book live and breathe and deliver its unique mystery and magic all on its own.

For the Love of It

Sadly, read-aloud is disappearing from our schools and classrooms. It's being squeezed out and forgotten in favor of busyness and less effective but more direct instruction. But reading aloud to your class has the power to instill a love of reading like no other earthly strategy. It's your one guaranteed academic success connection with every student, no matter how much they may be struggling.

Furthermore, when they *want* to read because of the joyful example you set, they progress at a much faster rate than if reading is treated as a series of banal skills they have to apply every time they open a book.

So bring the joy back. Find time for read-aloud every day. Defend it as your one sacred non-negotiable. Unburden your students from having *to do* something and just allow them to savor the story. Let it tingle down into their pores.

Your goofy, toothy BFG impression, your down-home narration of Charlotte's web, your determined Atticus Finch closing argument. This is what they'll remember. This is what will alter their view of learning and school and inspire them to become good and voracious readers for the rest of their lives.

PART FOUR:
Instruction

31

How to Create an Independent, Motivated, and Mature Class

WHEN TEACHERS FIRST IMPLEMENT an effective classroom management plan . . .

- By teaching and modeling it in detail.
- By following it exactly as it's written.
- By being consistent day after day.

. . . they're often shocked by how peaceful their classroom becomes. The respect, the contentment, the quietude. The smiles, the thank yous, the calm energy. It's like having a whole new class.

But there is danger lurking.

You see, at the first sign of peace, it's all too common to start believing the lie that you're not doing enough. The silence of independent work, in particular, has a way of making teachers uncomfortable and raring to help out.

So, without considering the impact, they burst through the sacred cocoon of concentrated work and begin micromanaging students. They interrupt to offer hints, suggestions, and advice. They rush over and kneel down in response to every look of mild frustration and every hand raised. They assist and handhold and coddle, all the while undermining a critical part of the learning process and removing what students crave—and need—most: Freedom and responsibility.

The students, in turn, begin believing that they really do need your help for every little this and that. Hands go up all over the room and they quickly lose confidence in their ability to listen, learn, and do for themselves (learned helplessness). This causes boredom, irritability, low motivation, and the desire for you to personally reteach individually what you taught the entire class just minutes before. And although a faithfully followed classroom management plan will still keep a lid on things, their dissatisfaction will manifest itself in sneaky, off-task, and behind-the-back misbehavior.

Work-habit expectations should be spelled out for your students, without a doubt, as well as the tools they need to do the work successfully. But once these are established, you must cut your students loose. *Really cut them loose.* Send the message that independent work, whether individual or in groups, is truly independent. Be reluctant to rush over to provide what they can work through all on their own. Allow them to make many of their own choices and decisions and wrestle with whatever you place before them.

Give them the space they need to take ownership of their work, and their imagination, their energy and passion, and their intrinsic motivation will kick into high gear. Teach interesting and inspiring lessons. Provide everything they need to succeed. Check thoroughly for understanding and allow for every question. *Teach them well.* But then get out of their way.

Shift 100% of the responsibility for doing the work over to your class while you fade into a corner to observe and take in the big picture. Work on devoting more and more of the school day to independent work, projects, creative endeavors, etc. and less of the day to directed teaching.

Directed teaching is still important, mind you. In fact, it's critical that you become an expert in delivering lessons. But you must continually push the envelope on what your students can do for themselves. *This is learning.* This is how they develop and thrive and become empowered to chart their own course. This is what prepares them for success in a rapidly changing world.

Take more of you out of the picture, and you'll discover your students becoming staggeringly more mature, independent, and responsible. Their motivation, focus, and on-task behavior will increase tenfold, and they'll become persistent, self-directed problem solvers—even, and especially, the most challenging among them.

Your classroom management plan will still be there, obscured in the mist and watching over your students. But they'll hardly notice it anymore, because the joy of learning will take center stage.

32

How to Ask for and Receive Your Students' Attention Within Two Seconds

THE ABILITY TO ASK for and receive your students' attention is crucial. It's crucial because it saves precious learning time. It improves listening and performance. It allows you to give instruction anytime you need to and know that it will be heard and understood. It's also a sign of a well-run classroom.

The good news is that it isn't difficult to teach. It isn't difficult to groove the habit of politely responding to your call for attention within just a second or two. It can even be a lot of fun.

Here's how:

Step 1: Explain why.

It's good practice to explain why what you're asking of your students is important and worth practicing—in all areas of classroom management. This is a critical step in motivating them to not only go along with your expectations, but to agree with them on the basis that they make the classroom better and more enjoyable. This underscores the importance of *selling* not just your lessons, but anything and everything you want your students to be able to do well.

Step 2: Choose a signal.

Many teachers prefer train whistles, bells, and other manufactured sounds to signal for attention. And although these can work fine (as long as you remain in the classroom), your voice is a better option—because it will help develop the habit of listening attentively *whenever* you speak. It will develop the habit of consistently following your directions. It's an act of respect that will affect how they view you as the leader of the classroom. I recommend a simple: "Can I have your attention please?"

Step 3: Expect an immediate response.

The biggest mistake teachers make is allowing students more time than they need to respond. This is key.

When you frame your expectations in any terms other than immediate, your students will push their response time back further and further. The result is that you'll be waiting for their attention for increasingly longer periods of time until, at some point, they just won't bother. By expecting your students to be looking and listening to you before you even get to the end of your sentence, you'll never have to wait and rarely have to reteach.

Step 4: Model it.

Your students need to see exactly what giving you their attention looks like. To that end, sit at a student's desk and pretend you're working independently or as part of a group. You may also want to model other common scenarios like, for example, if they're up and getting a tissue or playing a learning game or rotating through centers.

Have a student play the part of the teacher while you engage in the activity. Upon their signal, stop what you're doing, turn your body to face them, and listen without moving. You're setting your expectations and thus should model *precisely* what you want. Adding *how not* to do it is also a good idea.

Step 5: Make practice fun.

Practicing routines and expectations with a spirit of fun will always result in greater buy-in. If you give your students something silly to say while they're pretending to work in groups, or engaged in other scenarios, learning will be faster, deeper, and longer lasting. Any nonsensical phrase will do. In the past, I've used "hey, hey, whaddya say," "murmur, murmur," and "blah, blah, blah," as well as a few others. The goofier, the better. Allow them to talk for 30 seconds or so, and then ask for their attention. Practice until they're able to be still, silent, and looking at you in less than two seconds.

Everything Easier

It's best to put the routine into play as soon as possible. Release your students to work on their group projects or gather science materials or anything else that causes them to get up and move about or talk to each other. Wait no more than five minutes, and then give your signal. If they don't get it right, if they don't respond exactly as they were taught, then run through another round of practice. Send the message that you really do mean what you say.

Nailing down this one routine is important because it makes *everything* easier and affects so many areas of learning and classroom management. It saves loads of time, improves listening, encourages group responsibility, and allows you to have instant and total control of your class anytime you need it. It's correlated with respect, politeness, and the pursuit of excellence, and it's worth getting right.

33

5 Ways to Respond to Wrong Answers

THERE ARE THOSE WHO believe you should never tell a student who volunteers an answer that they're wrong. And I certainly understand why. It can be embarrassing for them. It can feel like a rejection. It can discourage them from sharing again in the future. But there are times when you're looking for a particular answer or set of answers. And if you accept every response as equally valid, you're going to confuse your class.

Students need feedback. They need feedback to learn and grow intellectually. They need feedback to adjust, dig deeper, and narrow in on relevant themes, ideas, and solutions.

So when a student offers an erroneous or off-the-wall response to your query, the entire class needs to know. At the same time, however, you never want to discourage anyone who participates. So what's the solution? What follows are five ways to tell a student they're off the mark without embarrassing, rejecting, or discouraging them.

1. "How did you arrive at your answer?"

In this scenario, you're leading the student to discover on their own where and how they went astray. What's cool about this technique is that with your prompting and further questioning they'll often work their way to the answer you're looking for. It takes spending some time with one particular student, but it's worth the effort—as well as the lesson for the rest of the class.

2. "You're on the right track, but not there yet."

This is direct, but also encouraging. It validates the student's thinking and motivates them to go a little deeper. It also helps the rest of the class adjust and fine-tune their own thinking. It does, of course, have to be true. Otherwise, you'll send your entire class in the wrong direction.

3. "Interesting . . . it's not exactly what I was looking for, but tell me more."

This is a good response when you hear something you haven't heard of or thought of before. The student may have an idea or interpretation that is every bit as good as the one you have in mind, but just comes at the problem from a different angle. This has happened to me more times than I can count and illustrates how important it is to keep an open mind.

4. "I see where you're going, but remember that . . ."

In this instance, the student is way off, which is a sign that others are likely in the same boat. The best way to handle it is to offer a hint. Give them a clue, leave a bread trail, get them near the right path but not quite on it. It's better to have students wrestle a bit to get to a solution rather than guiding them too directly. It makes your lessons more compelling and naturally draws students into the excitement and challenge of learning.

5. "Thank you!"

This is a good way to go when many hands are in the air and you want to give everyone a chance to be heard. The way it works is that you would call on every student with their hand up and simply thank them for their answer, without ever commenting on whether any of them are correct. After working your way through the entire group, you would then reveal the solution you were looking for. This helps get more students involved and comfortable speaking and taking chances in front of the class. It also allows them to think through and modify their responses as they hear others share out. They still learn when they're off base, just not while under the glare of the rest of the class.

Be a Straight (But Compassionate) Shooter

Being honest with students is important. It's important to their social and intellectual development, their understanding of subject matter, and their academic progress. They *need* feedback. It's desperately important and an often-overlooked aspect of effective teaching.

But there is a fine line because we also want to encourage participation. We want them to feel safe enough to share their thoughts and ideas, no matter how wild or far out they may be. It makes learning fun and interesting and provides another layer of that secret sauce that causes students to love coming to your classroom every day.

The five responses above are proven ways to give genuine feedback without discouraging your students or throwing a wet blanket over good discussion. Add to them your gentle smile and encouraging tone of voice, and your students will continue to take risks no matter how wide of the target their arrows land.

How to Develop Good Listening

LISTENING IS *ALWAYS* a problem with a new group of students. You can count on it. Dwelling on it or complaining about it—as many teachers are wont to do—is a waste of time. The effective teacher is only concerned with what they can control. They're only concerned with the actions they must take to fix the problem. They meet their students where they are, and then show them the way up.

When it comes to developing good listening, the key is to speak in a way that will cause your students to tune in naturally. It's to make the act of listening to you a habit.

Here's how:

Stand in one place.
Standing in one place encourages your students to focus on you. It settles restlessness. It calms excitability. It removes many of the distractions and obstacles that interfere with listening, so that your highlighted voice becomes the most prominent stimuli in the room.

Soften your voice.
Most teachers talk too loud, believing that it helps students pay attention. But the truth is, it does the opposite. It makes them

passive and disinterested. It discourages them from looking in your direction and tuning you in.

Good listening is active. It requires students to lean in and follow your lips, facial expressions, and body language. It requires them to meet you halfway, to do their part, and to seek out meaning and understanding. The good news is that students do this intuitively when you soften your voice.

Stop repeating yourself.

Repeating yourself effectively removes any reason for your students to listen to you the first time. It grooves the habits of passivity and learned helplessness and weakens the power of your words. When you say it once, on the other hand, and expect them to get it, you encourage active listening, engagement, and relevant, pointed questions.

Cut the fat.

The fewer words you use, the better your students will listen. This underscores the importance of staying focused and on topic, of providing only what your students need to be successful. Keep your thoughts, fillers, and digressions to yourself. They only water down your message and lessen its impact.

Pause often.

Remembering to pause will give your students a moment to download the previous information. It also makes you more interesting. It infuses your words with depth, importance, authority, and when needed, drama. Pausing also allows you to check for understanding. In time, you can become remarkably accurate assessing comprehension simply by pausing to take notice of their expressions.

Focus on doing.

When speaking to your students, as much as possible, focus on what you want them *to do.* This is inherently more interesting to students and immediately activates their visualization powers. They automatically see themselves in their mind's eye doing what you ask.

Furthermore, successful classrooms are action-oriented. They're productive and active and locked-in on completing their objectives. Even lining up to leave the classroom is an opportunity to do something well.

It's About You

Many teachers can be overheard lamenting the poor listening in their classroom, but their solution to the problem rarely has anything to do with them. In their mind, their students are the problem. So they harp on the importance of good listening. They put their frustrations on display. They show a complete lack of faith in their students by incessantly moving about their room, increasing their volume, and repeating their words.

But good listening isn't about the students. It's about the teacher. It's about speaking in a way that leaves no one behind, that empowers students to tune in, that provides the conduit through which active, tenacious listening becomes a habit.

35

How to Give a Quick Direction Your Students Will Eagerly Follow

ONE OF THE GREAT frustrations many teachers share is that they can't seem to get their students to follow simple, procedural directions—at least not without considerable effort. In other words, they can't just say what they want and step back and watch it happen. Invariably, they find themselves refocusing off-task behavior, offering reminders and warnings, and guiding and cajoling students through something they should easily be able to do on their own.

And you can't model everything. You can't write a list of steps on an easel or open the floor for questions every time you give a direction. You don't always have an extra five minutes, much less one, to get your students lined up, split into pairs, or pulling materials out for a lesson. There just aren't enough hours in the day.

To be most effective, and to avoid ending each week wrung out and pondering a career change, you need to be able to give a quick direction, whether a previously practiced routine or not, and *know* it will be followed to a tee. What follows is a simple, four-step method of giving directions that will empower your students to follow them without hassle or wasted time.

Step #1 – Take advantage of the awkward pause.

After asking for and receiving quiet attention, most teachers pause a single beat before providing directions. It's a natural rhythm of speaking that students have grown accustomed to. So much so that they often use the moment as an opportunity to turn their attention elsewhere.

This near-Pavlovian response can be a major reason students appear lost and in need of your help. To combat this phenomenon, simply pause an extra beat or two—or until it begins to feel awkward. This catches students off-guard, breaks up the learned response, and causes them to keep their focus and attention on you and your message.

Step #2 – Know what you want.

It can't be stressed enough how important it is to have a vision, or moving picture in your mind, of precisely what you want your students to do. Too many teachers begin speaking with merely an idea or impression of what they want, which causes them to hem and haw and muddle their message with digressions, qualifiers, and other extraneous information.

When it comes to giving directions, brevity is king. Pare your words down to the barest but critical minimum. Offer a direct path from their seats, or wherever they happen to be, to the fulfillment of your vision. This doesn't mean, however, that you'll skimp on details. It means that you'll provide just enough input for success, but no more.

Step #3 – Use the 'go' strategy.

The 'go' strategy's usefulness is worth its weight in cashmere. To set it up, start your directions with the words, *"When I say go, you're going to . . ."* What this does is prevent your students from jumping ahead and falsely believing that they already know what you want from them.

In other words, it keeps them from moving on mentally or otherwise before hearing and downloading everything you have to say. Knowing that they can't proceed until receiving your 'go' signal frees them to really listen and form their own visualizations. Go is also a power word that initiates action, and will cause your students to get moving immediately.

Note: Be sure and take advantage of another off-rhythm, awkward pause before giving your 'go' signal.

Step #4 – Watch like a hawk.

A common mistake is to give a direction and then toggle your attention to other things. It's rare *not* to see a teacher do this. For example, they'll ask students to line up for a walk to the library, but then while trying to keep a blurry eye on things, turn to grab their keys, collect grading materials, etc.

What this does is remove two powerful modes of influence: your eyes and your presence—both of which have a direct effect on how well students follow directions. To that end, whenever you give a direction, stay in one place until it's completed—watching, observing, taking it in with an attitude that says, *"Show me."*

A Habit

Like all good learning behavior, following quick, procedural directions is a habit. It's a habit grooved through the clarity of your vision, the economy of your words, the rhythm of your voice, the attitude of your observing posture, and the expectation of excellence that flows unremitting from your every pore.

Your students are largely a product of what they've been exposed to before arriving in your classroom. Whether you size them up as being good or poor listeners is beside the point and has no relevancy to the future. Teachers often say things like, "My class this year just doesn't listen well," as if such a thing were set in stone.

The truth is, all students react predictably to certain teacher behaviors, and with the right strategies you can have the class of active, nimble listeners and doers that you really want—regardless of who is on your roster.

But you have to commit yourself to what *really* works in the classroom. You have to build for yourself a comprehensive picture of what exceptional classroom management looks like, from the way you carry yourself to how you respond to misbehavior to how you provide quick-fire directions. It's doable and within your grasp. You just have to take it.

36

How to Give Your Students Lengthy Directions

TELLING STUDENTS EXACTLY WHAT you want is good teaching. It seems obvious, but if you're unable to communicate what you want from your students, then they're never going to give it to you.

Too often when giving directions teachers begin talking before they're ready. They think out loud. They hem and haw. They hesitate. They appear unsure of themselves. *"Okay, um, let's see, here's what were gonna do…"* And they wonder why their students struggle to follow directions.

It's best to compose yourself first, decide what it is you really want your students to do, and then give it to them straight. *"When I say 'go' I want you to stand up, push in your chair, and line up for lunch."* This is good. This is excellent. The teacher informs her students that she is going to use the 'go' signal, which improves listening and keeps them from moving too soon, and then tells them precisely what she wants—simple, direct, and effective.

But what if you need to give your students directions to be carried out over a lengthy activity? This can be a challenge for students and a major source of frustration for teachers. The students start out strong enough, but soon everything falls apart. They forget. They get confused. They lose motivation. They become distracted. They start goofing off and misbehaving. It can make you want to run screaming for the parking lot.

To be an effective teacher, to keep your students on-task and to encourage independence, you must be able to give unforgettable directions.

Here's how:

Step 1: Make your directions a story.

Your students will pay close attention if you make your directions sound like a story progressing from beginning to end. This is easy to do if you picture one of your students working their way through each of the tasks you want them to complete. Stories are powerful and can make mundane directions come to life for students—especially when they see themselves in the story.

Step 2: Use "going to" to spark visualization.

To insert your students into your directions/story, use the words, "going to," as in, *"First, you're going to pick up your materials from the front table. Then you're going to…"* When students hear "going to" they begin picturing themselves actually doing it. "Going to" is a memory device that causes students to create a moving picture in their mind. It's also predictive. They take it as fact that they'll indeed be able to do everything you ask them—without your help.

Step 3: Include anchors.

As you walk your students through your directions, add a few simple but insignificant tasks along the way. For example, you might say, *"When you finish writing your hypothesis, you're going to run out and touch the basketball pole on the playground."*

Silly tasks like this act as anchors along a memory map for your students. The novelty and goofiness has a way of helping them remember the path that leads from the beginning of the activity to the successful end. It's also a lot of fun.

Step 4: Act out your directions.

Detailed modeling can be impractical for lengthy, multi-step activities. But you can always act out what you expect without ever leaving the front of your classroom. Use your body and facial expressions to dramatize the steps you want your students to take. It provides additional support for their visualization and helps them to better picture themselves completing the tasks you place before them.

Step 5: Use a winding path as reference.

On an easel or SMART Board, draw a winding path of boxes. In each box write a one or two-word reminder for your students to refer to. Each box represents a task, leading to a successful finish.

This supports the idea that the activity is a story and they're the lead characters. The last box should refer to the final anchor, a fun way to culminate the completion of the activity. For example, after your students record the final results of their science experiment, they hold their journals triumphantly in the air and say, "I did it!"

Step 6: Hang responsibility on their shoulders.

Before releasing your students to begin, ask, *"Is there anyone who doesn't know exactly what to do from the moment I say 'go' until you finish the activity? I want to know now. I don't want to find out during the activity that you don't understand."* By being proactive and asking if anyone *doesn't* understand, you effectively put the onus of speaking up on your students—saddling them with a greater feeling of responsibility to do it right.

Step 7: Increase the challenge.

When you first try this new way of giving directions, you may only have a few tasks, or steps, on your path. But as your students get better, and as they grow more independent, you'll be amazed at what they can do.

Bring it On

Great teaching doesn't have to feel like hard work. You don't have to strain and stress to be effective. You do, however, need to be able to communicate with your students in a way they understand. For most day-to-day classroom business it's best to be direct and straightforward with what you want. But for multi-step directions that take time to complete, you must create a story for your students.

Many teachers place giving individual help at the top of their priority list and don't give a second thought to how they provide the directions—which creates needy, dependent students whose first inclination is to look to their teacher rather than relying on themselves.

But when you can provide unforgettable directions, when your students can *see* what you expect from them and picture themselves doing it, they'll rarely need your help. And as you test them and push them with more and greater challenges, they'll develop into capable, independent students who will look back at you with eyes that say...

Bring it on.

37

Why Silent Modeling Is a Powerful Strategy

DONE RIGHT, MODELING HAS the power to teach your students virtually anything you want them to be able to do, and in a way they won't soon forget. The problem, however, is that most teachers don't model very well. They gloss over details. They rush through important steps. They cut short what should be a thorough and engaging process.

They also tend to talk too much, adding information that only distracts students from learning.

One sure way to avoid these mistakes, while at the same time ensuring excellent instruction, is to model in silence.

Here's why:

It makes you more interesting.
When you take away your ability to talk, you naturally become more demonstrative and therefore more interesting to your students. Your body language, facial expressions, and movements—out of sheer necessity—become compelling and communicative, attracting every eye in the room.

It purifies your instruction.

When you model in silence, you're assured of providing the purest form of instruction. You never have to worry that the wrong choice of words—or too many words—might taint, confuse, bore, or draw your students away from what you want them to learn.

It makes paying attention easy.

Although you still have to ask for attention before beginning any modeling exercise, once you have it, you'll have far less trouble keeping it. By narrowing the senses your students need to one, following along and understanding what you expect becomes easy.

It triggers an unforgettable movie in their mind.

When you model in a silent but highly detailed way—as if you're an actual student completing the precise steps you want them to take—they'll see themselves in their mind's eye successfully doing the same, which then sticks in their memory.

It allows direct access.

When you model wordlessly, all students—including second language learners—have direct access to your best instruction. No one is left to fend for themselves, ask a neighbor, or guess what you expect from them. Its simplicity removes impediments to learning.

It improves performance.

The best feature of silent modeling is that it improves performance. As soon as you release your students to practice what they've learned, you'll see the very moves, steps, and actions you demonstrated minutes before materialize right in front of you.

Better Teaching

Although silent modeling is good instruction, it's not a strategy you'll want to rely on every time you model. The truth is, including carefully chosen words and explanations can be additionally effective. The good news is that silent modeling will make you better able to do this. It will train you to speak more precisely, thoughtfully, and powerfully. It will shine a light on the importance of being highly detailed, yet simple and on target. It will keep you focused on delivering what your students need to know to be successful, and nothing more.

38

Why You Shouldn't Shush Your Students and What to Do Instead

WHEN YOU HEAR A teacher shushing students, it's a good sign things aren't going well. Behind tight shoulders, tired eyes, and index finger poised over puckered lips, you'll find a teacher struggling to keep they're head above water.

Shushing students to quiet them down is associated with shaky-at-best classroom management, chronically distracted students, and a mountain of stress. And because it becomes progressively less effective the more you do it, shushing promises more and more frustration as the school year rolls on.

Though not as self-sabotaging as yelling or scolding, shushing similarly makes teachers less likable with students. It also makes you look like you don't know what you're doing. Follow the steps below and you'll never feel the need to shush, hush, or plead for silence again.

1. Decide

Before starting any activity, decide the voice level you want from your students. It's important you consider this ahead of time. After all, if you don't know what you want, your students won't know either.

2. Model

Gather your students around you and model precisely the voice level you expect. Make your modeling exercise as detailed and realistic as you can. Your students need to see and experience what you want before it makes sense to them.

3. Practice

Ask your students to turn to the student(s) next to them and discuss their favorite movie or other topic using the voice level you modeled. Have them practice and prove to you they understand what you expect.

4. Observe

Good teachers observe a lot to make sure their expectations are being met. Start your activity and monitor their voice level closely—especially within the first several minutes.

5. Stop

If at any time their voice level gets louder than your expectation, instead of shushing your students, stop the activity by signaling for their attention. Do this whenever they exceed the level you've asked for.

6. Remind

After getting your students attention, remind them what the voice level expectation is and put them on notice that if anyone goes beyond it, there will be a consequence—as promised by your classroom management plan.

7. Enforce

Listening and following directions should be one of your classroom rules. As such, if any single student is unable or unwilling to keep his or her voice level as modeled and practiced, then enforce a consequence.

Note: With group discussions, voice levels tend to increase as students attempt to talk over the other voices in the room. If it becomes loud enough to distract individual groups, simply stop them, ask them to take a few deep breaths, and then restart the activity. Do not, however, enforce a consequence.

8. Standardize

Consider standardizing the speaking levels in your classroom. For example:

- Level 0: No Talking
- Level 1: Whispering
- Level 2: Small Group Discussion
- Level 3: Whole Class Sharing

Create a small poster for reference and before every activity say simply, "For the assembly today, we're at level zero."

Effective at Any Grade

It may take a week or two for your students to get the hang of it. But when they do, controlling noise and voice levels in your classroom is easy and becomes something you never really have to think about. Setting voice level expectations—for partner sharing, group work, browsing in the library, or just a walk across campus—through the super-effective one-two combination of detailed modeling and student practice works at any grade level.

And it's so much more effective than having no clear picture of what you want, no expectation to model for your students, and no sound strategy to modulate the voices in your classroom other than a great big ugly, "Shhhh!"

39

How to Keep Your Students Focused the Last Hour of the School Day

S O MUCH GOOD, QUALITY instruction is lost in the hour before dismissal. Energy supplies run low. Minds begin to wander. Misbehavior tempts. Despite your enthusiasm, rallying your students and pressing for new learning is a high-altitude climb compared to the sea cruise it was just hours before.

Indeed, for the better part of the teaching force, the final period is approached with cautious dread. *Who's going to disrupt the class this time? How often will I have to stop and wait? How many times will I need to remind and lecture and repeat myself?*

No matter how calm you begin the afternoon, no matter how energetic or determined, it rarely seems to go as well as you'd like. It rarely seems to match the clarity of thought and focus of the new morning. The truth is, the last hour of the day takes more out of you than the preceding hours put together. But it doesn't have to be this way. For there are a few simple steps you can take to ensure that the end of the day finishes as sharp and bright-eyed as it began.

Here's how:

Take a break.

A short break an hour or so before the end of the day is a welcome and refreshing balm for school-weary students. It shakes out restlessness, clears away cobwebs, and refocuses distracted minds for the final leg. It's a simple way to solve a big problem. What your break looks like, however, depends on what preceded it.

If your students have been sitting, particularly if they've been concentrating or engaged in independent work, then you *must* get them up and moving. Lead them in light exercise, stretching, or standing strength (yoga) poses. Anything that increases heart and respiratory rates will do.

Your class may also need to get some socializing out of their system. Give them a minute or so to walk over and say hello to a friend or make plans for after school. You're clearing the boards, so to speak, eliminating a major reason students lose attention during the final hour.

If, however, your students are wound up and full of excitable energy, perhaps they've just returned from recess or PE, then a different sort of break is in order—one meant to calm, refocus, and restore. In this case, ask your students to stand silently behind their desks, feet wide and hands behind their backs. Pause a moment and let their breathing regulate naturally. Then lead them in a series of long, slow breaths—in through the nose, out through the mouth, as the diaphragm extends and retracts.

Go ahead and reach above your head and stretch during the inhalation phase if you wish, bringing your hands down and in front on the exhale. Five to ten repetitions followed by another pause should do the trick in calming and rejuvenating restless minds and overactive limbs.

Lean heavily on routines.

It's critically important that you finish the school day—that is, the last several minutes—without chaos, confusion, or misbehavior, that your last connection with your students matches the purpose-driven start of the morning. This day-after-day expectation will help you avoid a mountain of headaches at dismissal. But that's not all. Surprisingly, it will also help keep your students engaged and focused from the early afternoon through to the end.

Well-performed routines, you see, act as bookends to periods of learning, ensuring that the goals, ambitions, and responsibilities of your classroom are never far from mind. In other words, there is always another expectation around the bend, another active responsibility to stay sharp and ready for.

To that end, be sure and teach, model, and practice precisely what you expect during the last ten minutes of the school day. Your students need to be purposeful and busy and held to a standard of excellence all the way up until the moment they leave your room. Done right, there should be limited talking and virtually zero guidance on your part. Your role should be primarily that of an observer, carefully verifying that the high-bar standards you set for them are met.

Finish in silence.

Have your end-of-day routine finish with every student standing behind their desk, silent, reflective, backpack looped over shoulders. Wait until all are looking at you. Then, while referring to the clock on the wall, ask for 30 seconds of silence. This safeguards a peaceful, pleasant ending to your school day and eliminates the yelling, pushing, and running misbehavior so common after dismissal.

It also gives you a chance to provide a final thought, note of humor, or word of encouragement to send along with them. Make eye contact with each student, one at a time, as a silent invitation to line up. After repositioning yourself to the front of the line, release them out into the world with an easy smile, to their families, their homes, and their neighborhood lives.

The Space Between

The teachers who produce the greatest progress in their students year after year aren't necessarily the most dynamic. They aren't always funny or interesting or outwardly inspiring. They don't all know how to play guitar and sing or draw like Bill Watterson. And their lessons aren't always earth shattering. But what they do better than most is keep their students on task. They keep them focused and motivated and encouraged to take academic chances. They get the most out of each moment—from morning bell to dismissal.

They've developed the classroom management skills to keep distractions, interruptions, and time-consuming misbehaviors to a scanty, bare minimum. They focus their attention not so much on the moments outside of the school day—the meetings, discussions, trainings, busy work, and other necessary teacherly duties—but on the space between, the moments they're alone with their students. The moments of pure, day-to-day inspiration. The moments of discovery, of relationships, of smiles and breakthroughs and thank yous.

For this is what it comes down to, simply this, and this alone. The space between.

40

How to Motivate Unmotivated Students

YOU PRAISE. YOU ENCOURAGE. You pep-talk, demand, and implore. But nothing seems to change. Trying and failing to motivate unmotivated students is a common frustration among teachers. It's a frustration with seemingly no real answers beyond the same old, same old.

Until today. Because I'm going to share with you a reliable way to begin improving the work habits of your most reluctant students—students with next to zero interest in their schoolwork. It consists of a single, honest strategy you can feel good about using.

But first it's important to note that when we talk about motivation, it's common to think in terms of something we do to try and *convince* them to work harder. In other words, it's our external doing—our cheering, persuading, rebuking, exhorting, or coaxing—that kicks them into gear. It's our direct action upon them that makes the difference.

But this approach rarely works with hard-to-reach students, which makes it all the more remarkable that this is exactly what you've been told to do. It's the stock recommendation from every counselor, administrator, or specialist you confer with. You're told to praise, encourage, reward, and repeat, all day every day.

True motivation, however—that which is internal and sustaining—doesn't develop through convincing. It isn't about ramped-up enthusiasm or flattery. It isn't about stiffer consequences. It isn't even about motivation, per se. It's about inspiration. It's about a form of inspiration that comes from within the student—intrinsically rather than extrinsically. It's about tapping into that bubbling, churning life-brew buried deep down inside.

The strategy I'd like to share with you has a way of slipping by well-fortified, heard-it-all defenses. It has a way of sneaking by the palace guards and climbing in through a window.

It has a way of activating the desire to succeed without trying to convince your students of anything. It's remarkably and predictably effective, and yet all that is required of you is your honesty.

The first step is to stop the flow of excessive and over-the-top praise. Stop pulling inert students aside for pep-talks and lectures. Stop talking them through what they're capable of doing for themselves. Stop trying to use your creative use of words to get them going. Counterintuitive as it may seem, this alone will get a great many unmotivated students moving. The idea of relying on themselves feels good, and they'll give more, sometimes much more, than when you were pushing and prodding them along. Keep notice of this, but say nothing for now.

In the meantime, you're going to keep a lookout for evidence of quality work, no matter how small. You're going to keep a lookout for that which impresses you based on their ability. But instead of praising them for it, instead of saying how proud you are of them or how impressed you are with their effort, you're going to make an observation about their *work*. You're going to give plain and honest feedback about the evidence you see on the page or screen.

"That's good work."
"That's a well-written sentence."
"That's a clever idea."
"That's exactly right."
"Your conclusion is spot on."

Now, it's important that it must be true. The least motivated in particular can recognize phoniness from a mile a way. Having been on the receiving end of so much it, they've become experts. It's equally important that you don't use the same over-the-top voice and manner you may have used when praising them in the past. Just look down at their work, say your piece, and move on. And when you do . . . when you turn and head down the aisle without looking back, their insides will begin to stir. Beneath bowed head and downcast eyes, the faintest whisper of a smile will cross their lips. They may even suppress a giggle, joyous and inexplicable.

They'll have experienced the first rumblings of pride—not in themselves, mind you, not the selfish variety one feels in comparison to others, but pride in the work itself. Pride in excellence for excellence sake. Pride in something bigger and more important than themselves.

Good work habits, attentiveness, production, etc. aren't so much a matter of discipline that must be hammered into disinterested students. Nor are they the manufactured ballooning of the self through false praise. Rather, they are the awakening and nurturing of *delight* in the work itself.

By truthfully pointing out quality when you see it, you spark their once dormant intrinsic motivational engine to life. You awake the sleeping giant. You set down a single block from which you can build the pyramids at Giza. When struggling to motivate students who have practically no interest in anything you place before them, instead of focusing on the person, focus on their work. And the person will blossom.

Note: This isn't a one-time strategy to get a particular student to finish a particular assignment. It's a long-term approach that gradually draws reluctant students into the joy of creativity, the flow of concentrated effort, and the deep, soul-calming satisfaction that follows every job well done.

The Key to Motivating Students

IT'S IMPORTANT THAT YOUR students know you care about them. It's important that they know you're there for them. It's important that they know you only want what is best for them. This is no small thing.

The teacher whose students believe this about them is far more effective than the scores of teachers whose students don't, because it makes *everything* easier. Listening, attentiveness, behavior, maturity, independence . . . few areas of social and academic development are left untouched by your ability to communicate a one-way, no-strings-attached care and concern for your students.

But there is one area in particular that benefits the most. It's an area many teachers struggle with. It's also an area that is among the most misunderstood, even—or especially—by school districts and colleges entrusted with training teachers. The area is motivation.

Just knowing that you have their best interest at heart causes students to trust you and believe in what you say. It causes them to buy into your vision for the class. Again, this is no small thing, because when students believe that your words are true, your words will *mean* something to them. They'll hit their mark. They'll have an effect.

"I believe in you."
"You can do this."
"You have everything you need to succeed."

Coming from someone they trust and admire, the right words spoken at the right time can light a fire under even the most apathetic students. When they're preceded by a clear, well-taught lesson, and the expectation that independent work really means independent, they can transform a classroom.

However, there is one more key ingredient. It's an ingredient that makes many teachers nervous, an ingredient few feel safe even mentioning among mixed, staff lounge company. It is this: You have to be willing to let your students fail.

That's right. Your students must know that you're not going to do a scintilla of their work for them. You're not going to reteach the same things over and over again. You're not going to kneel down and coddle them through their assignments. You're not going to pretend that inadequate work is acceptable just so a student can pass. They have to know that they're truly on their own. They have to know that without effort and commitment to the work, they may go down in flames.

In educational circles, there is a reluctance to allow students to learn hard lessons. It's become a badge of honor—as well as an expectation—for teachers to do more and be more for their students. Administrators encourage it. Professional development trainers insinuate it. The current culture of teaching embraces it. But it's a disaster—for both students and teachers. It saps the motivation from students. It fills them with boredom and indifference. It shakes their confidence to the core. It's also a major reason so many teachers are stressed, burned out, and seeking a career change.

The only thing students learn from a teacher who won't let them fail is helplessness. The only thing they learn is that they *can't*.

When there is a prospect of failure, however, when there is a real and present danger of defeat, students feel the satisfying weight of responsibility. It gives them purpose. It gives them challenge. It gives them energy, accountability, determination, and excitement.

When there is something at stake, their motivational engines turn over. Their eyes brighten and narrow. Their spirit lifts. They develop grit and the mindset that *they can get better at anything through hard work.*

This is motivation. It's borne of vibrant, compelling lessons, clear instruction, and a total and complete shift of responsibility from teacher to students. It's borne of a teacher who communicates unconditional love for their students. It's borne of welcome burden, true independence, and the very real possibility of failure.

PART FIVE:
Teacher Habits

42

5 Simple Ways to Eliminate Stress From Your Teaching Life

STRESS IS A KILLER. And not just physically. It can also ruin your teaching career. It can destroy your peace and happiness. It can affect your relationship with students. It can severely limit your ability to manage your classroom.

The good news is that there is a lot you can do about teaching-related pressure, strain, tension, and the like. Even if you're prone to stress, it doesn't have to be your everyday reality. In fact, with just a few simple strategies, you can eliminate it from your teaching life.

Here's how:

1. Decide.

One of the most powerful and effective ways to rid yourself of stress also happens to be the simplest. It's called the decide-first method. The way it works is just before your students arrive for the day, shut your classroom door and allow yourself a few minutes of uninterrupted silence. Close your eyes, take a few deep breaths, and clear your mind.

Once settled, you're going to make one very important and very conscious decision. You're going to decide that no matter what happens during the day, you're going to keep your cool—inside as well as out.

Even if a family of orangutans comes swinging through your door, you're going to remain as calm as a mountain lake. And amazingly, almost magically, you will. The first time you try it will be a revelation. But if you run through the same routine every day, being calm and composed will become who you are.

2. Say no.

Nearly every teacher would benefit by using more of this two-letter word. If fact, if you don't say no regularly, chances are that you're overworked and near the end of your rope.

Now, it's important to mention that I don't just mean saying no to taking on extra responsibilities or joining another committee. You may also need to say no to gossip, procrastination, microman-agement, busywork, and commiserating with negative colleagues.

Saying no can feel awkward or uncomfortable at first, especially if you have to tell someone face to face. But once you take a stand, you'll be shocked at how much time you have to focus on what really matters. You'll be shocked at how much better you feel and how favorably your students respond to you. The truth is, if you want to love your job, and be most effective, you must learn to say no often.

3. Accept.

So many teachers get worked up over things they have no control over—like new policies, programs, curriculum, etc. But why do this to yourself? When something new comes down the pipe, it's far better and less stressful to accept it straightaway and then turn your thoughts to how you can make it work for you.

You don't have the time, nor can you afford the mental energy or anguish, to ruminate, complain, or become anxious over *anything* that has been decided by someone above your pay grade. To do otherwise is unhealthy and self-sabotage.

I've found over the years that I can take just about anything and make it my own, find a workaround, or, if it isn't something I absolutely have to do, ignore it altogether.

4. Stop convincing.

Teachers who struggle with unruly behavior, disrespect, poor listening, and a chaotic room environment tend to rely on their ability to convince students to behave. Which, even if you're blessed with natural charisma and a silver tongue, is a losing proposition. Besides being ineffective, trying to counsel, question, scold, guilt, coax, manipulate, persuade, or otherwise find the perfect words to get students to behave is incredibly burdensome and the most stressful strategy you can use.

Instead, lean exclusively on your classroom management plan. Let it do the dirty work for you. So many wonderful things happen when you simply allow it to fulfill its intended purpose. Not the least of which is your peace of mind.

5. Shift responsibility.

One thing nearly all stressed-out teachers have in common is that they willingly, eagerly even, take on what are—or should be—their students' responsibilities. After teaching a directed lesson, they fail to shift full responsibility for actually doing the work (independent practice) to their class. Instead, they disrupt the learning process by reteaching what they just taught minutes before.

They interrupt with reminders, clues, and suggestions. They rush to the side of every student who shows the least bit of struggle. They don't allow their students to wrestle with the material, build academic stamina, or draw their own conclusions. They think that giving and giving and giving is what good teaching looks like. But it's not.

Micromanaging and over-helping very effectively produce learned helplessness. They dissuade listening and encourage dependence on you. They create a room full of needy, grabby students that make you want to run screaming for the parking lot.

You Can Do It

You can't be an effective teacher if you're laden with stress. It shortens your patience, mars your judgment, and weakens your ability to build influential relationships with your students. It also brings tense, negative energy into your classroom *that you can't feel,* but visitors experience the moment they walk through your door.

No matter who you are or where you teach, the simple changes above can help you eliminate stress from your teaching life. But it does take discipline. It takes forethought and commitment. It takes determination and the will to swim against the tide of what everyone else seems to be doing. But you can do it. The journey begins with one small, daily decision.

43

Why Staying Late After School Is a Mistake

F OR A SMALL MINORITY of teachers, staying late after school is a symbol of their dedication. It makes them feel as if they're doing everything they can for their students. It gives them a sense of pride. They like having their car the last one on the parking lot—and the reputation that comes with it.

Others stay late out of a sense of duty. They feel guilty heading home when their contract day ends. So they tinker and brainstorm and busy themselves to exhaustion. Still others stay late because they have so much to do. They're overwhelmed with planning and preparation and firmly believe they have no choice in the matter. They stay late to survive.

But all are under a false assumption. Because staying late after school doesn't make you a better teacher. In fact, it makes you worse.

Unlike many professions, to be most effective, you need to be at your very best every day of the week. You need to be *on*. You need to be rested and refreshed before greeting your students each morning. You need to be clear-eyed and quick thinking, patient and observant. And the only way to ensure this happens is to get away from it. It's to drive off the lot at a decent hour without a glance back. It's to create mental distance between you and your job. It's to leave school at school.

Now, many teachers will tell you that they can handle the long hours, that they're fine, that they've been staying late for years without ill effect. But would their friends and family say the same thing about them? Can they honestly say that they're as sharp—or as relaxed, giving, energetic, interesting, fun, etc—as they would be if they were better rested? The truth is, simply leaving earlier—sometimes a lot earlier—can remove a mountain of stress from your life and make you a better teacher.

But what about preparation? Are you suggesting that teachers are better off underprepared? Well, a couple of things. First, most teachers prepare inefficiently. They get distracted. They meet with colleagues more than they need to. They visit and chat and don't always get down to work. They also get caught in a trap called Parkinson's Law. Parkinson's Law is the tendency to expand a task in complexity and importance in relation to the time given for its completion.

In other words, if you give yourself an hour to prepare, *you'll use the whole hour* when in all likelihood you could complete the task in less than half the time. The law also states that when you give yourself less time you become more focused. Your concentration increases. The obstacles and uncertainties that would otherwise crop up never enter the picture. Thus, the product is better.

Second, many teachers struggle with what, exactly, they need to plan and how to go about it. So they sit and ponder. They start and stop. They fill the time with busy work instead of productive work. They end up with lessons that are bloated and directionless and that students struggle to understand. Learning how to cut the fat and narrow in on what's important is a lesser-known—and almost never talked about—key to effective teaching. It's one of the topics covered in my book *The Happy Teacher Habits*, along with other ways to head home early and start loving your job.

While planning, it's best to first choose *one thing* per lesson that you want your students to be able to do or know or perform, and then determine the simplest and most direct way of accomplishing it. Set a deadline, say half or two-thirds the amount of time you usually stay after school, then stick with it. Turn out the lights. Close the door. Walk swiftly to your car without looking back.

Go be with your family. Ride your bike. Meet a friend at the park. You'll be happier, less stressed, and far better prepared than you've ever been before.

44

An Easy Way to Keep Your Cool
When Students Misbehave

A
T SCM, WE'VE TALKED a lot about the importance of keeping your cool when enforcing consequences. We've covered how it helps ensure that the offending student takes responsibility for their actions. We've covered how it causes them to reflect on their mistakes. We've covered how it maintains, and even strengthens, your relationships with *all* students. Just knowing its supreme importance is the best defense against becoming frustrated or angry when students misbehave.

However, there is one piece of advice we slipped into an article a few years ago that resonated with a lot of people. For them, it was the missing piece of the puzzle. It was the one thing that made it all click for them. It was the one thing that freed them from getting worked up over misbehavior.

We've heard from so many teachers since the article was first published that I thought I should share the advice again. It's a simple analogy, but it helps clarify how best to hold students accountable.

The advice is this: When enforcing consequences, think like a referee. A referee's job is to make sure players abide by the agreed-upon rules of the game. That's it. They make no judgments or decisions of their own accord. They have a rule book that lays out the parameters of the game, and they pledge to follow it to the letter. They watch the action closely, and when they see a foul or penalty, they blow their whistle and apply the specified consequence. It's automatic, something they do without pause or timidity.

A good referee is defined by their calm and consistent adherence to the rule book—the purpose of which is to make the game safe and fair for all participants. When a good referee is in charge of a game, play is smooth, competitive, and representative of good sportsmanship. Fans hardly realize they're even on the court or playing field.

When there is an inconsistent referee, however, or when they insert themselves and their personal feelings and biases into the process, they lose control of the game. Play becomes sloppy and uneven. Players and coaches grow angry and frustrated. Fans complain and throw popcorn. As an SCM reader recently pointed out, the game becomes unwatchable.

In this one way, refereeing is similar to teaching. Teachers who are inconsistent and enforce consequences based on how the misbehavior makes them feel, who is doing the misbehaving, or the perceived severity of the misbehavior also lose control. Students grow angry and resentful. The classroom becomes noisy and chaotic. Parents complain and throw popcorn.

The best way to keep your cool when you notice misbehavior is to call 'em like you see 'em. As soon as a student strays from your rule book (classroom management plan), follow through like a referee in the Super Bowl. No hesitation. No Fear. No Anger. Because when you focus on being a good referee, not only will you have excellent control of your class, but keeping your cool will be easy.

45

How to Have Jedi-Like Classroom Management Powers

THERE EXISTS A QUIET cadre of teachers who can take over any classroom—out-of-control, disrespectful, or otherwise—and get the students under control, quiet, and working within minutes. They have a certain presence about them, a certain unmistakable quality or vibe that reverberates from one student to the next, signaling that business is no longer usual. Almost magically students sit up straighter, listen more intently, and show a level of respect their former teachers would scarcely believe.

This powerful, Jedi-like presence can only be described as the force of their personality.

It's an attitude, or state of mind, that elicits in students a strong desire to give their best. Upon asking students why they're so different around such teachers, the common answer is, *"I don't know why I behave so well for Mrs. Jones. There is just something about her that makes me want to be a better student."* But the strategy these teachers use to command such reverence is no Jedi mind trick. The truth is, those who possess this "force" simply think differently than most teachers.

Here's how:

They take full responsibility.

No matter where they teach, under what conditions they teach, or who their students are, these Jedi-teachers take responsibility for everything that happens in their classroom—even if a herd of Wookies were to come stampeding through their midst. By offering no excuses for themselves or their students, they become empowered like a great surging wave to transform lives, set hearts afire for learning, and inspire their students to the highest mountaintops.

They have unshakable confidence.

Because they're experts in effective classroom management, thoughts of failure, defeat, and uncertainty never enter their mind. They have such confidence in their ability to manage behavior that it manifests itself in everything they do. You can see it plainly in how they move, speak, teach, and relate to students. And it is this confidence that causes students to want to place their trust in them and follow them to the ends of the galaxy.

They believe in their students.

These remarkably effective teachers have a deeply entrenched belief in their students and their ability to overcome circumstances, rise above difficulties, and stare down the demons conspiring to pull them away from their dreams.

This isn't just what these Jedi-teachers believe, but it's part of who they are. It brightens their every smile. It secretes from their pores. And it glows like embers in their eyes. For them to think otherwise would be the ultimate betrayal.

They know their students will behave.

Teachers who struggle with classroom management often feel as if they're one rainy day, one school assembly, or one fire drill from losing control of their class. On most days, they merely hope their students will behave.

Jedi-teachers, on the other hand, don't do any hoping. Backed by a classroom management plan that works, they have the mindset that no matter what comes up, or how many interruptions, their students will behave. And that's just the way it's going to be.

You Can Do This

Extraordinary classroom management isn't the province of a lucky few. You don't have to have a certain upbringing or personality. You don't have to be early in your career nor especially experienced. You don't have to have a booming voice, a comedic wit, or a duchess' grace. Short or tall, reserved or outgoing, anybody can do this. *You can do this.*

But you have to believe in yourself. You have to be a student of effective classroom management. And you have to start thinking like the Jedi-teacher you want to become. Now go and do it, and may the force be with you.

How to Be Both Calm and Enthusiastic

A CALM DISPOSITION CAN SWEEP excitability right out of your classroom. It can improve listening and attentiveness. It can curb misbehavior and accelerate maturity. It can also make you a more effective teacher. But inevitably, whenever I write about its importance, the question of enthusiasm comes up. *"How can I remain calm while at the same time show enthusiasm?"* Well, a couple things.

First, it's important to point out that they're not mutually exclusive. Calmness, of the kind that permeates the classroom and rubs off on students, is more of an inward feeling than an outward appearance. So even if you're acting out a funny story, as long as you're relaxed on the inside, your students will take it in stride. They'll enjoy it and laugh along with you. It won't wind them up or cause misbehavior, especially if you've established consistency in following your classroom management plan.

Second, while being calm internally is always good, there are times when it's best to be enthusiastic and times when it's best to be *reserved*. And herein lies the confusion. Calmness is a state of mind and body that accompanies the effective teacher from morning bell to dismissal, whereas enthusiasm and reserve trade off throughout the day.

To be most effective, you'll want to save your enthusiasm for *directed lessons*. So when you step before your students to teach a particular objective, you're free to let it fly. You're free to perform and inspire to your heart's content. You're free to use your passion to captivate, delight, and pull your students mind, body, and soul into your lesson.

But the moment you transition to giving directions or providing information, it's best to draw down your energy. It's best to stand in one place, slow your breathing, and limit your movements. Talk in a softer voice and focus on clarity and accuracy. Provide only the essential details needed to do the work, fulfill the objective, or perform the routine successfully.

While the former captures interest, the latter narrows your students' focus on *what they need to do*. Many teachers get this backward. They clap and exhort and bounce around the room trying to coax students into doing what they want, including behave, but then all but fall asleep during directed teaching.

They drone on and on and repeat themselves again and again. They flatten their voice and deaden their personality. They lose their spirit. But they plow on ahead, never noticing that their students are wilting, nodding off, or turning their attention to more interesting pursuits—like misbehavior.

Exceptional teaching demands that you maintain a calm disposition throughout the day, which not only eliminates excitability, but sets in motion many other wonderful benefits. It also demands that you know when to show enthusiasm and when to be reserved. Get these right, and your teaching will be infinitely more effective. Your students will be happier and less inclined to misbehave. And there will be peace in your kingdom.

47

8 Things Teachers Do to Cause Boredom

WHEN STUDENTS GET BORED their minds drift. And while some settle on daydreaming, tile-counting, and general inattentiveness, other students are drawn to more, ahem, destructive pursuits. For where there is boredom, there is misbehavior percolating just under the surface, ready to pounce.

Although there is a lot you can do to counter the onset of boredom, understanding what not to do is the first step to avoiding its negative effects. What follows is a list of the most common things teachers do to cause boredom. By steering clear of these eight attention killers, your students will spend more time on task and be far better behaved.

1. Sitting too long.
Although it's important to increase your students' stamina for both paying attention during lessons and focusing during independent work, if they're made to sit too long, you're asking for trouble. Good teachers are observant and thus learn to know precisely when to switch gears and get their students up and moving.

2. Talking too much.

Students need room to breathe or they'll form an unspoken mutiny and turn your classroom upside down. Talking too much is especially smothering. It communicates that you don't trust them, teaches them to tune you out, and causes their eyes to glaze over. The more economical and concise you are with your words, however, the more attentive your students will be.

3. Making the simple, complex.

Many teachers misunderstand the oft-heard mandate for more rigor. They take it to mean that they need to make their instruction more complex, more involved, more verbose—which is a major reason why students *don't* progress. Our job, if we are to do it well, is to do the opposite. The most effective teachers simplify, break down, and cut away the non-essentials—making content easier for students to grasp.

4. Making the interesting, uninteresting.

Most standard grade-level subject matter *is* interesting, but your students don't know that. In fact, many assume, based on their learning experiences in the past, that it's boring. It's your job to show them otherwise. It's your job to give them a reason to care about what you're teaching. So many teachers just talk at their students, forgetting the most critical element: *selling* it.

5. Talking about behavior instead of doing something about it.

Teachers who struggle with classroom management tend to talk endlessly about behavior. They hold class meetings. They hash things out. They revisit the same tired topic over and over, much to their students' eye-rolling chagrin. Effective classroom management is about action. It's about doing and following through and holding students accountable. It isn't about talking.

6. Directing too much, observing too little.

Most teachers are in constant motion—directing, guiding, hand-holding, and micromanaging students from one moment to the next. This is not only remarkably inefficient, but it dampens enthusiasm for school. Instead, rely on sharp, well-taught routines to keep your students awake, alive, and responsible through every transition and repeatable moment of your day—while you observe calmly from a distance.

7. Leading a slow, sloppy, slip-shod pace.

Good teaching strives for a focus and efficiency of time, movement, and energy. The day crackles and glides cleanly from one lesson or activity to the next. As soon as one objective is met, it's on to the next without delay. Moving sharply and purposefully forces students to stay on their toes, their minds engaged. Boredom never enters the picture.

8. Failing to adjust.

Regardless of what you're trying to squeeze in by the end of the day, or how important it seems, the moment you notice heads wilting, you must make an adjustment. It's never worth it to plow through. Sometimes all your students need is a moment to stretch their legs or say hello to a friend. Other times, you'll simply move on to something else.

Learning in the Spotlight

The ability to concentrate over time is a critical and often-overlooked aspect of learning, and so pushing the time-on-task envelop is a good thing. But there is a fine line. And when students cross that line and into boredom, misbehavior is sure to follow. The good news is that by avoiding the common mistakes listed above, you can keep boredom at bay, and inspired learning in the spotlight.

48

Why Gentleness Is a Strong Classroom Management Strategy

THERE IS A COMMON misconception that you must have a big presence to be an effective leader. You must psych yourself up, throw your shoulders back, and move boldly among your students. Your voice must boom. Your walk must swagger. Your eyes must squint and narrow in on your charges.

While classroom presence is important, it isn't born of over-confidence, forcefulness, or aggression. It's born of gentleness.

Here's why:

Gentleness is respected.

21st-century students respond best to a calm, even-handed approach to classroom management. They appreciate honesty and kindness. They respect it, and thus, are quick to listen and please their teacher. The older the students are, the more this is true.

Gentleness lowers stress.

Without saying a word, a gentle presence removes classroom stress, tension, and anxiety. It soothes and alleviates excitability and distraction—which are two major causes of misbehavior. It equals a happier, more productive classroom.

Gentleness curtails pushback.

Enforcing consequences calmly and consistently diminishes the possibility that your students will argue, complain, or lie to you about their misbehavior. Instead, they'll quietly take responsibility.

Gentleness builds rapport.

When you carry yourself with a gentle demeanor, you become more likable to your students. In fact, it's an easy and predictable way to build powerful leverage, influence, and rapport, which makes *everything* easier.

Gentleness feels good.

Beginning each morning with a poised, easygoing manner will make you a lot happier. Inconveniences won't get on your nerves. Difficult students won't get under your skin. You'll be refreshed at the end of every day.

Gentleness Isn't Weakness

Weakness is when you lose emotional control. It's when you lecture, berate, and admonish students instead of following your classroom management plan. It's when you take misbehavior personally. Gentleness, on the other hand, is strong. It's capable and confident. It says that you're in control and that your students can relax and focus on their responsibilities.

This doesn't mean your lessons won't be dynamic and passionate. It doesn't mean you won't be enthusiastic or you won't demand excellence from your students. Gentleness isn't sleepiness. Nor is it afraid and cowering in a corner. It's a calm, reassuring approach to managing your classroom that communicates to every student that you're a leader worth following.

Martin Luther King Jr. was gentle. So were Rosa Parks and Abraham Lincoln. And so are the happiest and most effective teachers on Earth.

How to Talk to Parents
Who Just Don't Care

F
OR THE MOST PART, it's a misnomer. 99.9% of parents
love their children. They may have a misguided way of showing it. They may not sign one bit of correspondence from the
school. They may be uninvolved, negligent, or worse. They may
be preoccupied trying to get their own life together.

But few don't genuinely want what is best for their children.
The key to talking to parents who don't appear to care is to speak
to that part of them that really, really does.

Here's how:

1. Make contact.
The first step is to doggedly pursue making personal contact. Most
teachers will try the one or two phone numbers on file, but then
give up and send an unreturned email instead.

You must go the extra mile. You may have to call the company
or organization they work for. You may have to call neighbors
and cousins and friends of friends. You may have to wait and
speak to whoever picks up their child after school. Whatever it
takes to get the parent on the phone is worth doing. It can even
be life changing.

Most parents who are difficult to get hold of are never actually contacted. So when you go out of your way to surprise them at work or through a neighbor they're typically humbled and over-the-moon appreciative.

2. Treat them with royal respect.

The biggest key to tapping into that part of them that deeply cares about their child's welfare is to speak to them as if they've been voted parent of the year. Speak to them in the same manner you would a parent who cuts the crusts off the lunch bread and is front and center at every school event. Give them their dignity back.

This affectation of tone and expression is magic. Seldom have they been spoken to with such respect, and in response they'll rise to meet the subtle call to be worthy of it.

3. Remind them of their responsibility.

Somewhere along the line many teachers have acquired the awful habit of intimating—or outright commanding—parents to *do something* in response to their call. Many even condescend to make suggestions. But unless expressly asked, this oversteps your bounds. It puts parents on the defensive. It makes them feel an inch tall and all but guarantees that they won't speak to their child about your issue.

The most effective approach is to start with something positive and then kindly relay the facts. "I'm so happy to have your daughter in my class this year. She is outgoing and asks excellent questions. My concern is that she hasn't been doing her homework . . ." Be specific but maintain your respectful tone. Never allow your frustration to surface. Before hanging up, add the key line:

"The reason I wanted to tell you personally is because *I knew you'd want to know.*"

This is a gentle but powerful reminder that hits them directly in the heart. You can hear them sigh and melt on the other end of the line. Most will thank you profusely and request that you keep them posted. It's also a good idea to take the opportunity to invite them to your class or tell them about upcoming events.

A Profound Difference

Although it seems like a simple little thing, when you go out of your way to contact wayward parents in a non-judgmental way it almost always makes a profound difference. They start asking their child about their day. They inquire about behavior and take an interest in homework. They become more responsible. Combined with your faithful adherence to your classroom management plan, you'll see a change in their child as sure as the leaves change in fall.

The greatest reward, though, is the day they darken your doorway. They'll step in eyes wide, tentative and uncertain, at back-to-school night or to volunteer for a field trip. But once you bound toward them with a smile and a handshake, once they get comfortable getting to know the other parents and children, they'll glow.

50

How to Handle Parents Who Complain About Their Child Being Held Accountable

I N THIS DAY AND age, when you consistently enforce your classroom management plan, it's bound to happen. A parent approaches you to complain not about a particular incident, or their child's role in breaking class rules, but that their child was held accountable.

In other words, they're not denying the misbehavior. They're upset because their child was given a consequence. They don't like the idea of them in time-out or having lunch detention or any other mode of accountability.

It's a situation that is happening more and more among SCM readers. And it can be hard to know what to say.

Now, it's important to mention that parents who complain about accountability are often just frustrated that everything isn't going as swimmingly for their child as they'd like. It hurts them personally. It ruins their day. They become so attached to their own vision of their child's success, that they advocate letting them off the hook or giving them additional chances.

Although it isn't always easy, the best way to handle it is to just be honest. Here's how in three steps:

1. Be friendly.

No matter how irritated or upset a parent behaves, it's never a good idea to respond in kind. You'll only make things worse. It's best to yield, let them have their moment, and affect a gentle, kindly temperament.

Smile when you greet them, even if you're talking on the phone (it will come through), and thank them for speaking to you. Simple friendliness will help diffuse their frustration and send the message that you're competent, professional, and someone they can trust.

2. Listen.

Give the parent as much time as they need to express their feelings. Often, all they want is to be heard and know that you're doing the right thing for their child. So don't jump in. Don't interrupt or try to counter every point. Don't say anything at all. Just listen, nod your head, and show that you're interested in what they have to say.

When they finish, thank them again for bringing their concerns to you and being there for their child.

3. Give it to 'em straight.

The most effective response is direct and honest. Don't beat around the bush or hem and haw, but confidently stand your ground and be the same leader your students see everyday. Look them in the eye and say (still friendly):

"Every student in this classroom has the right to learn and enjoy school without interference, including yours, and it's my job to protect that right by enforcing a consequence, as stated in our classroom management plan, every time a student breaks a rule. If I were to let things go, if I were to allow students to interrupt the class without being held accountable, then I would lose control of the class and learning would suffer. Furthermore, fair and respectful accountability encourages students to take responsibility for their mistakes, which is healthy and keeps them from making them again and again."

Then briefly share something positive about their child or express how much you enjoy having them in your class. And that's it. Nothing else needs to be said.

Stand Your Ground

The idea is to show them that accountability is a good thing, that it's part of a good education that prepares them for success inside and outside of the classroom and well into the future. If you follow the steps above, then in all likelihood the parent will understand and appreciate the true purpose of your classroom management plan.

And if they don't? So be it. It isn't your concern. No matter how vociferously they complain, continue to be calm and pleasant as you walk them to the door. Just as you're consistent with your students, you must be equally consistent with parents. You're the teacher and the leader of the classroom, and that's just the way it is.

You're paid to make decisions that are *best for students*, first and foremost, that protect their freedom to learn in a safe, peaceful, disruption-free, bully-free environment. That protection extends to everyone and everything that threatens it, even their own parents.

51

How to Avoid Angry Parent Complaints

A T SCM, WE'VE HEARD horror stories about angry parents. Teachers have emailed us to share incidents of ranting and raving. They've shared how parents have interrupted their class and confronted them in front of students. They've told of parents who've stomped into the principal's office and even shown up at board meetings to try and get them fired.

In every case, it's in response to how the teacher handled misbehavior. And in every case, it could have been avoided.

Here's how:

Get parents on record.

During the first week of school, send home a copy of your classroom management plan. Include a page with a simple declaration that the parent has read and understood your plan. Ask for it to be signed and returned to you. The idea is to get parents on record of knowing full well the behavior expectations of the class and how students will be held accountable.

Review your plan.

In your correspondence regarding back-to-school night, be sure to let parents know that you'll be reviewing your plan in detail.

This way, you'll be on record as having given them an opportunity to learn more, voice concerns, or ask questions.

At back-to-school night, lay out your plan from beginning to end. Walk parents through the exact steps you'll take when a student misbehaves. Emphasize that the purpose of your classroom management plan is to protect every child's right to learn and enjoy school. Finish by promising to follow it to a tee. Be clear, speak confidently, and you'll rarely get even a single question. You will, however, have parents thanking you afterward.

Fulfill your promise.

Now that you've publicly made a commitment to safeguard your classroom from disruption, you must follow through. You must be consistent every day of the year. If you go back on your word, if you lecture, scold, or allow misbehavior to go without consequence, you open yourself up to complaints that are very difficult to defend against.

But here's the thing: Being consistent is made easier by your promise. You'll remember all those signatures, all those faces you met at back-to-school night, and you'll want to do right by them. You'll want to be worthy of their trust.

The Way It Is

If you follow the guidelines above, you won't get complaints. You just won't—even if not a single parent shows up at back-to-school night. However, if the unheard of happens and a parent does voice a concern, it won't be about you. It will be about your classroom management plan, which is non-negotiable. You'll politely explain that you'll continue to protect learning, safety, and contentment of every student in your class. And that's just the way it is.

In 99.9 percent of cases, parents complain because their child's right to learn is being trampled on. They complain because their child has to endure an environment of chaos. They complain because instead of having an impartial way of holding students accountable, the teacher berates and reprimands or ignores misbehavior altogether.

The secret to avoiding parent complaints is to lay bare the ins and outs of your classroom management plan from day one. Get everyone on record—parents, students, and even yourself.

Then do what you promise.

PART SIX:
Difficult Students

52

How to Handle Students Who Lie and Deny

WHILE OBSERVING YOUR CLASS gather materials for a science experiment, you notice a student kicking the heels of the boy in front of them. But because you're in the good habit of letting misbehavior play out, you decide to watch a bit longer before jumping in. You see the boy turn and ask the student to stop. After a brief pause, however, the student resumes the practice. You mentally record every move, and as soon as they sit down, you approach.

The student sees you coming and before you can even get all the words out ("I saw you kicking Darren and—"), they begin aggressively denying. "That's not true! I didn't do anything. Oh my gosh! I wasn't kicking anyone." Your first inclination is to refute the student's claims, to prove that you're right and they're wrong. *"Yes, you were. I saw you with my own eyes from across the room. Now stop lying and take responsibility for your actions."*

But doing so would draw you into an argument. It would put you on equal footing with the student. It would turn into a your-word-against-theirs battle royal. This is a common situation, one so many teachers find themselves stuck in every day. It's frustrating. It's stressful. It puts you at odds with your students and turns you into the ogre you never wanted to be.

The good news is that it's entirely avoidable. All of it—the lying, the denying, the arguing, and the stress. It's all avoidable using the following three steps:

1. Know the truth.

You should only approach a student to give a consequence when you *know* the truth. This underscores the importance of letting misbehavior play out, of eliminating any plausible deniability, of leaving no doubt who is responsible and what rule was broken.

If you're unsure, then get to the bottom of it first before confronting the student. This step alone will save you a mountain of headaches. Still, like the teacher above, it isn't always enough to avoid a confrontation. The next two steps are crucial.

2. Enforce.

With the truth on your side, there is no reason for debate. There is no reason to ask why. There is no reason to allow the student to lie to you or deny their involvement. Simply approach and say, "You have a warning because you broke rule number three."

Most often, that's all you need to say. However, if you're uncertain they know what misbehavior you're referring to, then you can add, "You were kicking Darren while getting science materials."

3. Move on.

After delivering your consequence, turn on your heel and walk away. Nothing else needs to be said and waiting for a response is an invitation to argue. Because you've taught, modeled, and practiced your classroom management plan thoroughly, the student knows exactly what this means.

They know you have them dead to rights. They know that in your classroom, rules that protect learning and enjoyment are sacred and nonnegotiable. They know that arguing, denying, or complaining is fruitless. The only thing left for them to do is take responsibility.

Avoidance Is the Key

Many teachers contact us wanting to know how to respond when students lie, yell, throw tantrums, refuse to go to time-out, or engage in other aggressively willful behaviors, and we gladly cover these topics. But the trick is to avoid them from happening to begin with. The three-step strategy above is a perfect example. By calmly—even matter-of-factly—delivering your consequences with truth on your side, and then walking away, you avoid the behaviors students have used since time immemorial to sidestep accountability. You avoid the arguments and protestations. You avoid the deceptions and shocked faces. You avoid the manipulations that have worked with so many other adults in their life, including teachers.

And here's the thing: When you do what you say you will, when you handle accountability fairly and consistently, when you show your students how much you care by safeguarding their right to learn and enjoy school without interference, chaos, or drama . . . they'll love and respect you because of it.

53

Why You Shouldn't Try to Convince Difficult Students to Behave

I T HAPPENS EVERY DAY in classrooms from Fresno to Kathmandu. The teacher pulls aside their most difficult student for a private meeting. Sometimes it's a lecture. Sometimes it's a pep-talk. Sometimes it's to threaten or praise or question like a trial lawyer. But in every case, the teacher is trying to *convince* the student to behave. They're trying to use their tone of voice and creative use of words to inspire a change in behavior. And although there can be some immediate improvement, it never lasts. In fact, the likely result is a worsening of behavior. Because, when you try to convince students to behave, you're showing how much it means to you. You're letting them know how much their behavior affects you, stresses you out, alters your mood, or gets under your skin.

And in so doing, you give away your leverage. You weaken your influence. You cede the upper hand in the relationship and give your most challenging students the power to make or break your day. This isn't something they consciously think about, mind you. It's just human nature. When there is a crack in the foundation of leadership, however small, your students will fill it—or wrest control of the classroom right out of your hands.

To turn around your most difficult students, and actually *change* their behavior, you must never show how much it means to you. Unless you need private information, it's best to refrain from pulling them aside for one-on-one chats.

Instead, if they misbehave, follow your classroom management plan. Enforce your consequences calmly and matter-of-factly. Pretend you don't give one whit whether they misbehave or not. Deliver your news and then walk away as if nothing happened. Never let them see you sweat.

If, however, you notice real improvement in behavior, then let them know it directly and honestly.

"Now that's how you do it!"
"I thought you were great today."
"You can't do any better than that. Way to go!"
"I knew you could do it."

In the meantime, strengthen your leverage, influence, and leadership presence through your steadiness—your day-after-day kindness, consistency, pleasantness, and humor.

Show them, prove to them, through your smiles and hellos and friendly banter that every day is a new day. Be the leader they need, not the weak-kneed groveler they don't. Your refusal to pull them aside to woo, plead, coax, cajole, or manipulate communicates loud and clear that you believe in them. They really can do it. It's an undeniable truth that they'll see in your eyes, your face, and your entire being every day of the week.

And it will change them.

54

A Radical Way to Transform Difficult Students

S O YOU HAVE THIS student who disrupts your class every day. They're a constant annoyance. You spend more time dealing with them than any ten students put together. You think about them in your off hours. You talk about them with your spouse. They get under your skin like nothing else.

You hold them accountable and cycle them through your consequences day after day, but to little avail. They improve for a couple of hours, maybe a day, and then it's right back where they started. It's wearing on you, stressing you out, and affecting your enjoyment of the job. You've tried everything, so it seems, and now you're at your wit's end.

I'm going to offer you a radical solution. It's a solution that at first glance seems almost too simple, but it sets in motion a series of changes within the student that can have a profound effect on their behavior. It takes a bit of willpower, along with a mental hurdle you'll have to cross. But the results can be startling. The way it works is that you're going to *change how you think* about the student.

You see, as the year goes on and you get more and more frustrated, negative thoughts about them are bound to seep in.

Perhaps they've been there from the get-go. It's normal, and understandable, to feel this way. Resentment can even grow outside of your conscious awareness.

Before you know it, this one student, and how much they get on your nerves, is consuming your thoughts.

Well, the big secret is that *they know how you feel about them*, even if you've done your Meryl Streep-best pretending otherwise. Because it's something you can't hide. Although you may have never raised your voice, scolded, or lectured this student, the subtle ways in which you talk to them and behave around them let's them know your true feelings. They can see it in your eyes, your tight smile, and your closed body language. This isn't something they're necessarily consciously aware of. But they know.

Children are astute, even psychic, judges of how adults perceive them. Far more than we give them credit for. Think of a time when you've met a baby or toddler for the first time, but weren't in the mood to coo and ah. Despite your best acting efforts, and biggest, goofiest smile, they could feel your disingenuousness. You can see it in their eyes. This is true no matter the grade level you teach.

When there is an absence of mutual likability between you and your most challenging students, you lose nearly all of your leverage to influence their behavior. Because you don't matter to them. What you say, want, request, and advise doesn't matter to them. It's just an annoyance. So what's the solution? How do you get them to listen to you and start behaving like just any other student in your class? You choose to like them.

You make a conscious decision that, no matter what they do or how they behave or how many times they disrupt your class, you're going to see only the best in them. You're going to change your thinking—which really is a choice, nothing more. In fact, once you set aside your negative feelings about them, once you shrug off your resentment and decide to like them, you'll find that it isn't so difficult after all.

And here's the good news: Improvement will happen fast. Students are quick to forgive and eager for someone to look up to. They're eager for a leader they can trust and follow and believe in. So when you choose to see the best in them, when your smile is genuine and your interest in them is real, it changes everything. And they'll like you right back.

It triggers the Law of Reciprocity and causes in them a desire to please you and behave for you. Your words of praise, encouragement, and honest disappointment will mean something to them, deep down, where change happens. *This* is leadership.

Few teachers have a genuinely good relationship with their most difficult students. But those who do are able to inspire lasting improvement. They're able to make an impact on those who've been written off, labeled, and merely tolerated. They're able to do something no other teacher has been able to do. And so are you.

By making one radical, beautiful choice.

55

How to Handle Students
Who Give You Attitude

E YE ROLLS, DEEP SIGHS, melodramatic body language . . . they're responses to teacher requests or reminders (i.e. "Please put your backpack away.") that aren't quite disrespectful, but darn close. Sometimes they're accompanied by a sarcastic "Sorry!" or "Oh my gosh!" They're delivered indirectly and out of frustration and are usually not malicious. They do, however, have a way of getting under the teacher's skin.

So much so that here at SCM we've heard from dozens of teachers wondering how best to handle it. There is something about student "attitude" that drives teachers up the wall. At the very least it can put you in a bad mood, especially because you're just trying to be helpful. You're just trying to save the student from trouble or help them avoid a mistake. (*And the thanks I get is an eye roll?*) It's hard to bite your tongue. It's hard not to be pulled into an argument or respond with a rip-roaring lecture.

So what's the solution? Well, this may surprise you, but following your classroom management plan isn't the best response to a single act of student attitude. For one, I don't believe it rises to the level of disrespect. Although it often feels like it, it isn't directed at you. Rather, it's an act of personal frustration.

Enforcing a consequence, then, often makes things worse, deepening the student's frustration and discontent. There is also a far better way of eliminating it from your classroom. Before we get there, however, it helps to remember that all of us have experienced similar frustrations, which is my second point.

Whether trying to renew your driver's license at the DMV or waiting for food at a restaurant, we all know how easy it is to roll your eyes at the clerk or server or let out a long sigh—despite knowing deep down that they're just trying to help.

Yes, "attitude" comes far too easy with some of our students, no doubt about it. But understanding that they're having a bad moment is the first step to turning their attitude around and ensuring that it doesn't happen again.

It's a very simple strategy, but extremely effective. The way it works is when a student rolls their eyes or gives attitude about something you've said, you're going to smile at them. Not a mocking smile, by any measure, but a lighthearted gesture of understanding. An accompanying chuckle may also fit the moment. It should only last a second or two, and then you'll move on without a word. It's such a small thing, but it has an amazing way of breaking tension, diffusing escalating emotions, and allowing the student to recognize their overreaction.

It communicates that you don't give directions because you like bossing people around—which, based on their experience in the past, is how many students view teachers. You do it because it's helpful. You do it because it's right. You do it because it's best for them and for maintaining a learning environment where they and their classmates can thrive.

The very first time you try it some students will smile right back at you or even laugh at themselves. But the real power of the strategy is when you make it your default response to *all* acts of attitude and personal frustration.

You'll begin noticing a greater acceptance of your requests, reminders, and commands and an eagerness to follow them without complaint. There will be less tension in your classroom and more joyfulness. The only danger is to be sure you're clear on the difference between a student having a bad moment and blatant disrespect, which must always be followed by a consequence.

Student attitude is a display of frustration that has nothing to do with you. The most effective response is one that shows that you've been there, you get it, and it's okay to laugh at yourself and the minor annoyances that follow us every day of our lives. In time, you'll eliminate virtually all attitude from your classroom and replace it with acceptance, eagerness, and smiles.

56

How to Hold Difficult Students Accountable

A READER RECENTLY ASKED A question I've gotten a lot over the years. *"How should I hold difficult students accountable?"* It's a topic I hadn't yet covered specifically because the answer is so simple and direct: Just like everyone else. You calmly approach the student. You deliver the news. *"You have a warning for breaking rule number two."* Then you walk away.

It's a way of enforcing consequences *with all students* without causing friction or resentment. The result is that as long as you've taught your classroom management plan thoroughly, and you're consistent, your students will look inward rather than pointing the finger elsewhere.

They may not be happy about the consequence, but they'll reflect on their misbehavior. They'll take ownership and responsibility and resolve not to make the same mistake again. But the reader added an interesting twist to his question.

You see, over time he had established a good relationship with his more challenging students and was concerned about disrupting their "growing identity as well-behaved students." So much so that he was walking on eggshells around them. He was nervous about holding them accountable and damaging the relationship.

It's a valid concern. Because, when a difficult student is in the midst of transitioning into the well-behaved student you envision them to be, it's a tenuous time. One stern lecture or burst of anger from you could send them in the opposite direction.

So, even though you can't go wrong with holding them accountable in the manner described above, there is one thing you can do to ensure that you aren't misunderstood. There is one thing you can do to safeguard your all-important relationship and send the message that receiving a consequence from you isn't personal. All it takes is a simple change in phrasing. As you approach the student, it's important to remember to be especially calm—even pleasant and easygoing. Take a few deep breaths if you have to. There is no hurry. When you get their attention, make eye contact and say:

> *"Hey Anthony, I really appreciate how well you've been doing, but I have to give you a warning for breaking rule number two."*

You're still delivering your consequence. You're still being clear and consistent. But you're doing it in a way that acknowledges their improvement. It's a subtle but effective way of communicating that you're just doing your job and that it in no way affects how you feel about them. The key phrase here is *I have to*. It reinforces their image of you as a leader to be trusted, as a person of integrity they can count on to do what they say they're going to do.

I've used this strategy hundreds of times and the reaction is almost always the same: The student will look down, nod their head, and say, *"I understand."* You may also receive an apology, although it usually comes at the end of the day.

Both are proof that your relationship remains strong and influential. They show that the student is indeed on the right track and that their improvement is sure to continue. It's a simple little change, hard to believe it could make much difference. But for those few students on the cusp of great and enduring change, it can mean the world to them.

How to Handle a Student Who Yells at You

RECENTLY, I RECEIVED AN email from a teacher who was yelled at by a student. Her class had been in the middle of a learning game, and everything was going smoothly. Or so she thought. The students were playing by the rules. They were having fun and enjoying each other. They were playing cooperatively. In fact, she was thrilled with how well the activity was going.

But then, out of the blue, a student stood up and accused her of favoring one team over another. When she tried to explain, he began arguing with her. When she defended herself and her decisions and assured him that she would never do such a thing, he became furious. He began yelling, pointing his finger at her, and calling her a cheater. It was an ugly scene, and the teacher was left shaken and unsure of how to handle it.

This isn't the first email we've received on this topic. And it won't be the last. Confrontations like this are happening more frequently. In this day and age, students seem more aggressive when they feel slighted and less willing to listen to another point of view. Furthermore, many have never had anyone show them, or model for them, what respect looks like. This underscores the importance of first deescalating the situation—in order to ensure your safety and the safety of your students—before teaching a life-lesson the offending student won't soon forget.

Here's how:

1. Delay.

The instant you recognize—or think you recognize—a student becoming angry, your singular goal is to calm them down and avoid confrontation. In the case above, the moment the student stood up, the teacher should have gone into de-escalation mode.

The best way to do this is to delay. *Do not respond directly to the student's complaints.* Doing so will only make things worse. Instead, stay cool and relaxed, pretend it's no big deal, and say:

> *"It's okay. I understand what you're saying. I can see how you might feel that way. I promise I'll fix it, but let's finish the game first."*

Then move on as quickly as you can. Go ahead and let the student complain a bit longer if they wish or get in a last word. Delay, delay, delay, and they'll calm down.

2. Fix.

You are under no obligation to explain yourself or your decisions to any student who speaks to you or approaches you disrespect-fully—nor should you. It only encourages more disrespect.

However, after the student settles down, it's smart to set the record straight by clarifying your rules, protocols, or procedures related to the game or activity *to the entire class.* This allows you to defend your decisions as the teacher and leader of the classroom while at the same time fulfilling your promise to "fix it." Get to the point, be brief, and provide facts only.

3. Enforce.

Your classroom management plan should include an addendum that allows you to skip the warning stage and jump directly to a more appropriate consequence. Any incident of brazen or continued disrespect should be met with your strongest consequence—which may include an extended time-out for elementary students or detention for high school students—plus a notification of parents.

The behavior should also be documented and, if it was in any way threatening, aggressive, or potentially dangerous, then officially referred to an administrator.

Only after the student has forgotten about the incident, which may be much later in the day, or even the next, should you approach, deliver the news of your consequence, and then walk away.

4. Review.

Students tend to repeat the behavior they see from others. This is one reason why a class can get out of control so quickly. Therefore, it's important that you review your rules again a day or so after the incident. Severe misbehavior can act as an agent to *improve* behavior and politeness class-wide. Whenever you have a dramatic incident or a particularly bad day, you should view it as an opportunity to teach a valuable lesson to the entire class.

Focus on your rule concerning disrespect. Be sure and define once again what it looks like and reiterate that it won't be tolerated, that you won't allow anyone or anything to upset the experience of being a member of your class. Finish your review by reminding your students that the goal of your classroom management plan is to safeguard their right to learn and enjoy school and your right to teach great lessons.

Limiting Contact

As counterintuitive as it may seem, the less contact you have with the offending student, the less likely a similar incident will happen in the future. Pulling them aside to counsel, patch things up, force an apology, or convince them of your point of view will only weaken your leverage and influence. Let accountability do your talking for you.

By not taking their disrespect personally, but instead keeping your cool and following through on your promise to protect learning, your respect in the eyes of *all* your students will grow. The offending student, especially, is often changed by the experience. So much so that they'll begin treating you with reverence and even admiration.

When you then show them—through your simple kindness and no-hard-feelings acceptance—what grace, forgiveness, and true respect looks like, you'll forever change how they view the world.

58

How to Handle Class-Clown Disruptions and Disrespect

THERE IS NOTHING WRONG with a class clown. In fact, students gifted with a clever sense of humor can be a wonderful asset to your classroom. They can be another ingredient in the mix that helps you create a learning environment students love being part of. The truth is, the most effective classrooms laugh. They laugh and joke and enjoy each other much more than most teachers realize. As long as it's done within the confines of the class rules, humor should be encouraged and even led by the teacher. It makes your ability to influence behavior that much stronger.

But when a student steps outside those boundaries to deliver an ill-timed one-liner, it can have the opposite effect. It can pull the entire class off task. It can cause silliness and excitability. It can encourage others to do the same. It can also make the teacher feel as if it was done at their expense, especially if it happens during direct instruction. After all, in one fell swoop a funny remark can undo the time and effort that went into creating a captivating lesson or engaging activity.

It's natural to be offended, to take it personally, to glare daggers in the student's direction or cut them off with a biting rebuke. But an angry reaction will only make matters worse. It will extend and deepen the interruption. It will bring stress and negativity into your classroom. It will ensure a slow return to focused work and cast a dark cloud over the rest of the day. It will also put into motion an antagonistic relationship with the offending student, one that can be difficult to overcome.

So, how should you handle it? Well, it's instructive to look at the situation from the student's perspective. The truth is, when they make a silly comment, *their intention isn't to humiliate you.* How you feel about it emotionally isn't even on their radar. They just want to crack up their classmates. That's it.

Now, it's important to point out that such outbursts *are* disrespectful, no doubt about it. A willingness to interrupt your teaching shows a lack of regard for you as well as their classmates. But the class clown is only thinking of themself and the attention the moment can bring them.

So you must tread lightly. You must approach the situation shrewdly and strategically rather than impulsively. You must handle it in such a way that minimizes the disruption, yet at the same time holds the student accountable, restores respect for you, and lessens the chances of it happening again. Reacting in anger won't cut it, not even close. In fact, the most effective reaction is no reaction at all.

Don't frown. Don't tense. Don't even sigh. Just stand in place and wait for the moment to pass. Wait for movement to cease. Wait for silence to be restored. Let the weight of disrupting the sacredness of teaching and learning in your classroom dawn on the offending student. Let them realize of their own accord that they just interrupted, disrespectfully, the teacher they like and admire. Let the entirety of the moment hang in the air as a message to every student. You see, when you let the elephant in the room just stand there, alone and awkward and shuffling its feet, the lesson becomes *powerful and meaningful* to everyone in the class. Especially to the offending student, whose witty quip now rings hollow and absurdly out of place. When the moment is right—and you'll know when—calmly take a step or two toward the student, deliver your consequence matter-of-factly, then turn and get on with your lesson.

In this way, you safeguard your relationship with the disruptive student. You restore, and even increase, respect for you. And you all but remove the chances of it happening again. In less than 60 seconds you're back to work.

As if it never happened.

59

How to Handle Disrespectful Students Who Don't Know They're Being Disrespectful

A STUDENT POINTS THEIR FINGER inches from your face and teasingly says, "I'm mad at you. That homework last night was hard!" Or . . . a student raises their hand and *commands* you to "Tell John to stop bothering me." In either case you're uncomfortable with the way you've been addressed. It's given you pause, and you're unsure how to respond.

On one hand, neither student appears to have any malicious intent. From their tone of voice and body language, it's clear they don't realize they're being disrespectful. On the other hand, they *are* being disrespectful, no doubt about it. So how should you proceed?

Should you follow your classroom management plan as it's written and risk causing confusion and resentment? Or should you ignore their disrespect on the grounds that they don't know any better and risk more of the same behavior? What follows are seven steps that will allow you to handle this surprisingly common situation with grace and sensitivity, while all but removing the chances of it happening again.

1. Move on.

The first step is to quickly move on from the incident while neither endorsing nor condemning their behavior. The key here is to keep your cool, avoiding any outward expression of anger or disappointment. A thin smile and a nod of the head will usually suffice.

However, if applicable, you may have to calmly tell the student that you'll speak to them about it later.

2. Pull aside.

After the incident is forgotten (30 minutes is a good rule of thumb), pull the student aside for a quick word. At SCM we typically don't recommend private meetings with students regarding their behavior. In this case, however, it's warranted.

3. Avoid confrontation.

There is no reason to question the student or force assurances from them. Your sole purpose is to educate. You see, when you tell students "this is the way it is," they readily accept it. It's when you browbeat them into telling you what you want to hear that they become defensive and argumentative.

4. Recount and inform.

Recount the exact actions and words the student used that triggered your instinct that their behavior was disrespectful. Then simply inform them that it crossed the line, that it isn't okay to speak to a teacher the way they might a friend or sibling.

5. Model the alternative.

The next step is to illustrate how they should have addressed you. Model it for them so they know exactly what you mean. No matter how irritated their behavior made you feel, be sure and maintain a helpful demeanor. It's key to ensuring that it doesn't happen again.

6. Pause.

A short pause will give the student a chance to speak if they wish. You'll often get an apology. If you don't, however, or if the student clams up, that's okay. It's not important that they admit their mistake. Your meeting isn't a form of accountability, and it shouldn't be construed as such.

7. Make a promise.

Finish your conversation with a promise that if it happens again, you'll enforce a consequence. By patiently setting the record straight, the student will walk away from your two-minute meeting with a greater appreciation of you and a fuller, more meaningful understanding of respect.

Defining Disrespect

Disrespect appears to be on the rise—particularly among younger students. It's important, however, to determine if the disrespect is intentional or a misunderstanding of the definition. Sadly, as surprising as it may seem, due to poor home and neighborhood influences many students just don't know any better. And enforcing consequences for behavior your students don't understand to be wrong will jeopardize your relationship with them. It will cause friction, distrust, and resentment and increase rather than decrease the chances of it happening again.

The good news is that body language and tone of voice will always tell you whether to enforce a consequence immediately or pull the student aside for a brief lesson. This underscores the importance of teaching this particular topic thoroughly in the beginning of the school year. If you model the most likely scenarios—like those above, for example—and define for your students precisely where the line is, then instances of disrespect, intentional or not, will be few and far between.

Why You Shouldn't Respond When
a Difficult Student Has a Good Day

W HEN A DIFFICULT STUDENT has a good day
it's normal to want to reward them for it. You've just
witnessed behavior you've been hoping and praying for
all year, and you want to seize the moment. You want to make it
special and memorable. You want them to feel good about their
accomplishment and start believing that they really can do it,
that they really are capable of following your class rules. So you
rifle through your cabinets looking for an award or certificate
you can present them. You dig into your prize box. You rush to
their side and excitedly share how happy and proud of them you
are and how wonderful they behaved that day.

And it all feels so good and so right. But the truth is, the
best response you can offer a difficult student after a good day
is no response at all.

Here's why:

Good behavior is its own reward.
When you reward students for good behavior they become exter-
nally motivated. They begin to view anything and everything

positive they do as work they deserve to be paid for. They become blinded to the truth that good behavior is a reward unto itself.

It's an expectation that is beneficial to them and to the community they're a part of. For difficult students in particular, this healthy perspective is hidden from view in a forest of excessive praise and ginned-up awards. It's a "do this and get that" economy that is manipulative and hurtful to their long-term success.

It's empowering.

Real and lasting change only happens when difficult students are intrinsically motivated to behave. In other words, when it comes of their own volition, and not because they are offered—implicitly or explicitly—something in return.

When difficult students are allowed to experience success without it being purchased, the quiet satisfaction vibrates deep within their internal motivational engine. It gives them the warm feeling of being a regular and valued member of your classroom, rather than an outcast who needs bribes and special attention just to get through the day.

A True Reward

Although they may smile, they may even be excited to receive a cool pencil or toy or special recognition, if you look closely you'll find sadness behind the eyes. Because it cheapens their good day. It puts a price tag on the priceless. It replaces the intrinsic with the extrinsic. That isn't to say that you should shun or ignore difficult students after a good day. You'll just treat them like everyone else.

You'll joke with them, smile at them, and enjoy their company. You'll support the wonderful feeling of being a regular student—just one of the girls or boys. You'll allow them to experience a reward that is honest and abiding and can't be purchased for any price. You'll restore their self-respect. You'll remove the labels they carry with them like so many overstuffed backpacks. You'll pave the way for the rest of your class to see them in a new light.

But most important, you'll empower them to start seeing themselves differently. Instead of a weak constitution, tossed about, manipulated, and cheaply bought, they can begin envisioning their future. They can see possibilities where before there were none. They can feel their dreams power up and surge like a tidal wave.

Maybe a day or so later you'll catch them looking at you—knowingly, appreciatively. No words need to be exchanged. No explanations offered or needed. For how do you describe the view from the summit of Mount Everest?

But you want to acknowledge the start of something special, of true improvement in behavior. So you approach and reach out your hand, and they reach back and shake it.

How to Handle Needy, Grabby, Dependent Students

THEY MATERIALIZE IN FRONT of you, demanding your attention. They pull on your sleeve and tap on your arm. They barge into your personal space, interrupt you where you stand, and begin talking before you even have a chance to acknowledge them. They tattle. They complain. They dramatize. They need you to fix their problem *right now*.

Needy students can be a major source of stress, without a doubt, but here's the thing. They aren't difficult to handle.

In fact, with the right approach, you can not only discourage such behavior, but eliminate it from your classroom altogether.

Here's how:

Don't lean down.

When you lean down toward needy students, you encourage their behavior. You encourage more drama and more interruptions in the future. Simply by staying upright, you're communicating your boundaries. You're gently reminding them that you teach an entire class, not just one student.

Now, if there is truly an emergency, your teacherly powers will surely let you know. In which case, leaning down to get more information is appropriate.

Don't respond.

In the immediate moments following their interruption, it's important that you don't respond. It's okay to look in their direction to let them know you hear them, but refrain from opening your mouth. Give them a chance to catch themselves, to rethink their behavior, to consider a more mature and polite way of speaking to you. If a class rule was broken, after pausing, enforce a consequence. *"You have a warning because you left your seat without permission."*

Don't show concern.

Needy, dependent students tend to overreact. They tend to make mountains out of molehills. They tend to rely heavily on the adults in their life rather than themselves. This tendency will only worsen if you validate their behavior. It will only worsen if you stop what you're doing, allow them to interrupt you, and show concern. While this is a natural reaction from a caring teacher, it's detrimental to their social and emotional development—not to mention your peace.

An Easy Fix

The level of dependency in your classroom is directly related to how you respond to it. This is a key issue, because if left unchecked, a culture of neediness will infiltrate everything you do. It will affect every lesson, every activity, and every routine. It will make your life infinitely more difficult and stressful and cause you to be a less effective teacher.

The good news is that it's an easy fix. Combined with a reluctance to coddle, over-help, and reteach individual students again and again, the guidelines above will have a remarkable effect on your classroom.

They will turn your students into doers and problem-solvers, independent learners and lean-in listeners. They will build confidence and competence and even strengthen character. But you have to stop doing what comes naturally, and instead, do what works.

How to Handle a Student Who Questions You With Disrespect

T'S AMONG THE MOST requested topics we've ever had. How do you handle a student who questions you, your decisions, or the way you run your classroom? How do you respond when you *know* their motives are less than pure, when you know they're just trying to get under your skin? Or worse, trying to get the class to turn against you.

The "question" usually comes out of left field, catching you off guard. It's almost always public, confrontational, and in the form of a challenge:

> *"Why can't we just leave our seats when we feel like it?"*
> *"Why do we have to be silent while we work?"*
> *"Don't you think it's mean to make us do our essays over and over again?"*

With more than a tinge of attitude, the student is clearly being disrespectful. But because it's cloaked in the guise of a question, enforcing a consequence straightaway would likely only add fuel to their fire. It would only prove their point—in their mind, anyway, as well as in front of the class—that you're mean and unfair.

On the other hand, it's hard to know what to say. It's hard not to come across as angry, flustered, or defensive. So how should you handle it?

Here's how in three easy steps:

1. Defer.

It's best not to respond to their question—at least not right away. Instead, defuse the tension in the room by deferring your answer to a later time. Say, "I appreciate your question, but now's not a good time. Let's finish this lesson first, and when I get a chance, we can talk." Then move on as if nothing happened. Refuse to give them the forum to air their grievances or drag you into an argument in front of the class.

2. Wait.

Wait at least twenty minutes before approaching the student. This way, you give them a chance to calm down and rethink the manner in which they posed their question. Waiting also shifts control of the situation to you. During this time, it's important to formulate a simple, direct, and honest response that demonstrates how the rule or policy in question benefits *them*—as well as every student in the class.

3. Approach.

Avoid pulling the student aside for a private chat or otherwise making the situation bigger and more important than it is. Just approach them where they are, smile, and deliver your prepared line:

"You must raise your hand before leaving your seat because it protects every student from disruption and is best for learning."

"We must be quiet while we're working because every student has a right to concentrate without interruption."

"Rewriting is an important part of the writing process that will improve your essay and make you a better writer."

Follow up with another smile and a quick, "Now get back to work." Then turn and be on your way.

The Importance of Why

The three-step strategy will defuse tension and hostility, allow you to take control of the situation, and provide an effective response to their question. It will reinforce the message that you know what you're doing and that you base your decisions on what's best for them. Handling it this way is honest. It's clear and true and reestablishes the roles of student and teacher. It also effectively eliminates future challenges to your authority.

However, it's important to note that the incident itself is a sign that you're not adequately explaining the *why* of what you do. The *why* is so, so important. Because when your students know why they must work silently or raise their hand or rewrite essays, or follow any other rule, policy, or procedure, they're far more willing, and even eager, to go along with it.

What Difficult Students Desperately Need But Rarely Get

N O, IT'S NOT ATTENTION. For the most part difficult students are given far too much attention. Learning how to spend less time on difficult students will do both you and them an ocean of good. In fact, it's among the critical first steps to restoring their dignity and common pride in being a regular, contributing member of your classroom.

No, what your most challenging students need most is your honest feedback. They need you to tell them the truth about their successes and failures. They need you to look them in the eye with compassion and tell them like it is—warts and all.

Most difficult students are subjected to a baffling combination of false praise and angry criticism. Teachers volley between the two like Federer and Nadal. And neither provides the feedback these students need to understand how they're really doing. So they flounder about, misinformed, pinning their future on an inaccurate picture of what it takes to succeed in school and the wider world.

On the one hand, they're gratuitously praised for what are common expectations. They're told they did a "great job" because they sat quietly during a lesson. They're given a "way to go" for *not* hitting or pushing at recess. They get prizes and accolades and awards for doing what they're supposed to do, for accomplishing the barest, low-bar minimum. On the other hand, they're often harshly and personally criticized for their mistakes. They're given umpteen lectures, scoldings, and reprimands that leave them defensive and resentful and unable to see even a kernel of truth to the criticisms.

They're left floating in a sea of faulty mixed signals, tossed about by flattery and disparagement. Are they wonderful and special because they can go an entire morning without being sent to time-out, or are they unlikable and worthy of scorn because they can't? They're neither, of course. Yet these are the predominant messages they hear about themselves day after day, year upon year.

The Gift of Truth

The only way difficult students can begin climbing out of the hole they've dug themselves is to know how deep the hole is. They need someone to step forward and consistently reflect for them how they're *really* doing. They need the one thing, the one precious gift, that will show them the way up and out of the hole and standing on their own two feet.

They need the truth, spoken and unspoken. The unspoken truth is your fair and consistent classroom management plan. Its action-based accountability clearly communicates that their behavior has strayed from the habits necessary for success in school. And because it isn't personal or hurtful, it's a truth that gets through, that's taken to heart, that points the finger of responsibility directly and solely at them.

As much as possible, let your plan do your talking for you. If, however, you feel the occasion to address a student individually, your words should be spoken plainly and calmly and only in those rare moments when a phrase or two can make the truth more impactful.

"That isn't good enough."
"You're just not making it right now."
"You're better than that."

Then be on your way. Let the truth do its good work. Give your students an opportunity to self-examine and ponder and feel remorse all on their own. Let them make a promise to themselves to do better.

And when they do well? Saying nothing at all is often the most truthful and powerful way you can respond—because it communicates loud and clear that right behavior and attentive habits are expected and not worthy of special recognition. An honest word or two, though, or a heartfelt, non-verbal gesture, based not on temporary improvement, but on real change in behavior, can mean the world to them. It's a simple acknowledgement that you notice and approve.

Think of your most difficult students and the scores of conflicting, untruthful, and unreliable messages they've been given over the years. Surely it reaches into the thousands. Decide right now to restore this false picture to the original, imperfect, and beautiful masterpiece that it is. Give them the gift of truth and nothing but. For it is the one thing that can pull them off the dizzying roller coaster ride of false praise and harsh criticism.

And place them firmly on solid ground.

How to Handle Students Who Misbehave Behind Your Back

I T CAN BE ESPECIALLY frustrating. You're working with a group or helping an individual student. Perhaps you're walking the perimeter of your classroom, observing and looking over shoulders. Then you hear a burst of chatter and giggling just out of your view. You look up or turn, but nothing seems amiss, at least, nothing blatant.

But you know there were students misbehaving. You know there were students off task and taking advantage of a moment when your back was turned. You even know who it was, pretty certain anyway, because you can see it on their faces. They're now looking at you and others are looking in their direction.

But you hesitate to enforce a consequence because you aren't absolutely sure. Plus, they know you didn't see them, which could embolden them to lie and deny. So what should you do?

Well, because behind-the-back misbehavior often feels like it's at your expense, and therefore disrespectful, many teachers get fired up about it. A seed of anger rises inside them and they can't help but confront those they believe are responsible. So they stomp over and question. They warn and threaten. They pit one student against another to try to coerce a confession. All to make sure that it doesn't happen again.

But this is a remarkably stressful approach that risks building a wall of resentment with students who may or may not even be guilty. Besides, there is no guarantee you'll get to the bottom of it. You will, however, bring tension into your classroom and may very well have nothing to show for it—with the offenders getting away scot-free. When students misbehave behind your back, or just out of your view, it takes a subtle, even sly, approach to identify the culprits and hold them accountable. It takes pretending that you didn't even notice their misbehavior.

You see, if at first you do nothing at all, if you show no reaction or change in routine or behavior, it's a surefire guarantee that they're going to do it again—usually within seconds.

But this time, you're going to catch them in the act. You're going to use your teacherly sense to choose the right moment to shoot a hidden glance in their direction. You're going to heighten your awareness, finely tune your hearing and peripheral vision, and position yourself so you can anticipate their antics. You may even move further away from them or turn your head the other way.

Eventually you will catch them in the act. You will be able to enforce a consequence without stress, drama, or the prospect of having to prove their misbehavior. No arguing, battling, or threatening, just pure accountability.

It's your job to see misbehavior, to protect every student's right to learn and enjoy school. Vigilant supervision is a prerequisite of effective classroom management. But there are times when the pelota gets by the goalkeeper. And when it does, you can still catch them. You can still follow through. You can still prove that you really do have eyes in the back of your head.

65

How to Stop Students From Breaking the Same Rule Again and Again

S O YOU HAVE THIS student. Let's call her Brittany. And Brittany frustrates you to no end. Because despite holding her accountable, she continues to break the same rule over and over. Oh, she may hold off for a few days, a week perhaps, but it inevitably happens again. She pushes a classmate in line. She runs out to recess. She leaves her seat without permission. Whatever the behavior, the scene plays out the same. But the habit never breaks.

Now, it's important to point out that if you're inconsistent, if you don't enforce a consequence every time a rule is broken, then this is the first order of business. Inconsistency is the number one reason students continue to break the same rules again and again. Shoring up this one area will eliminate most, if not all, recurring misbehavior.

There are, however, those rare students whose impulsiveness gets the better of them. Despite knowing that you'll hold them accountable, they can't seem to help themselves. They see a clear pathway out to recess, for example, and the moment overwhelms them. Their eyes light up. Their heart begins racing. They think, *soccer, soccer, soccer . . . freedom, freedom, freedom . . . fun . . .*

laughter . . . friends! The excitement of the moment so dominates their thoughts that nothing else occurs to them. They blurt out the answer. They shoulder a classmate out of line. They race to the playground without looking back.

So what's the solution? Well, if you're a regular reader of SCM, then you know that pulling Brittany aside to discuss her persistent misbehavior is a mistake. Questioning, lecturing, forcing assurances, and the like is too personal. It will only alienate her, create friction between you, and ultimately lead to more problems and misbehavior. What she needs is much simpler than that. What she needs is an interruption of her impulsive habit. What she needs is a reminder.

Now, in and of itself, offering reminders isn't an uncommon strategy. Having learned what moments, activities, or times of day trigger a student's misbehavior, many teachers do this. The problem with the strategy, however, is that it singles her out. The other students can see you and often hear you reminding Brittany, which makes her feel different.

No, you're not scarring her for life. But what you are doing is labeling her as incapable.

You're telling her in a very subtle way that she is unlike other students, that she alone needs a reminder in order to control herself. Before you know it, she is telling herself, and even friends and family members, that she has trouble controlling herself. It feels like a permanent condition she can do little about. Although it may work in the moment, which is why the strategy is so common, your reminder is actually creating, reinforcing, and cementing a limiting belief she has about herself. It has the opposite of the intended effect.

So how can you give Brittany a reminder in a way that helps her break the habit once and for all? You remind the entire class.

Although Brittany may be the only one who pushes other students while jostling to get in line, you remind everyone. You restate your expectations for the routine and then position yourself where every student can see you watching them carry it out. In time, whole-class reminders combined with faithful accountability will break Brittany of her impulsive rule-breaking.

This doesn't mean that you have to give reminders every time you transition or begin a routine. You'll only give them during those moments throughout the day that seem to trigger her misbehavior. Brittany, and other students like her, don't need to be pulled aside for lectures, threats, and warnings. They don't need your pep-talks, glares, or whispered admonishments. They don't need to be singled out at all. They just need one simple reminder given to the entire class.

66

Why You Shouldn't Pep-Talk Difficult Students

T HE STUDENT STANDS WORDLESSLY, eyes averted, still smarting from yet another backslide as the earnest teacher softens the blows of the student's many transgressions. Listing positive attributes, offering reassurances, buoying spirits, the teacher seeks the slightest spark of understanding, the slightest recognition indicating that his (or her) pep-talk is hitting its mark, getting through, doing some good. He cajoles, he praises, he soothes and emotes . . . he all but tap dances around the student with a hat and cane. It's a time-consuming, mentally taxing exercise.

But he keeps at it, week after week, because he's been led to believe that with the right words and inspiration, he can transform his most challenging students. It makes sense. It feels right. It should work. But pulling difficult students aside for pep-talks, particularly in response to recent misbehavior, will not only delay real and lasting improvement, but it can cause behavior to worsen.

Here's why:

They've heard it all.

Most difficult students have a history of misbehavior reaching as far back as preschool. Add the near-constant flow of pep-talks over the years, and you have a group of students who have heard it all. Thus, they've become jaded and adept at tuning you out or telling you what you want to hear. For them, these moments are more embarrassing than they are uplifting.

Pep-talks lack meaning.

Unless a student has taken an improving step of their own accord, then little of what you say will make a difference—because it lacks basis, proof, or truth and therefore any meaning. It's a sand castle at low tide. A brief acknowledgement based on real improvement, on the other hand, can have remarkable power.

You give up your leverage.

When difficult students see how desperate you are for them to improve, you hand over much of the leverage you need to help them change their ways. Because they know how much it means to you. They can see it in your eyes and smell it on you from a million miles away. They know they have you over a barrel and can ruin your day whenever they wish

It labels them.

Whenever you spend extra time and attention on difficult students, you're essentially telling them that they're different and less capable. This is a powerful message that reinforces what most difficult students already believe about themselves. Frequent pep-talks intensify this false belief by communicating one thing above the static of your hyper-encouragement: that misbehavior is who they are and not merely something they've done.

Less Attention, More Dignity

Through all their misbehavior, silliness, and brazen disrespect, most difficult students shuffle through their day with an anvil around their neck. And pep-talks based primarily on the teacher's desire for a more peaceful classroom only add to their burden, stoking the fires of resentment, pushing them deeper into their shell of scarred differentness, and urging them on to more frequent and more severe misbehavior.

What they need most from you is their dignity. They need you to allow them to begin feeling like just another member of your classroom. They need the freedom to make mistakes and accept the consequences, the freedom to experience remorse and disappointment, and the freedom to feel the intrinsic determination to do and be better—all of their own accord and on their own terms.

So does this mean that you'll never interact with difficult students, that you'll never acknowledge their victories or failures? Not in the least. Carefully timed, small, private, and subtle moments of truth, in response to lessons *already* learned through fair and compassionate accountability, or through bona fide steps in improvement, can be life changing.

Eye contact and a nod from across the room, a knowing smile and a fist bump, a note folded over and waiting on their desk . . . these authentic moments between you mean the world to students labeled as "difficult." They ring like a bell through the night, penetrating the heart and filling with hope. Remembered for a lifetime.

67

How to Handle Aggressively Disrespectful Students

I OFTEN HEAR FROM TEACHERS who in long missives describe awful behavior towards them. They describe angry, argumentative, and aggressively disrespectful students. Students who tell them off and *try* to disrupt and sabotage their class. Students who roll their eyes and refuse to look at them or listen to their directions.

They go on to talk about how nothing works. How every day with 10-20% of the class is a battle. How behavior is getting worse, not better, and that these particular students don't care a whit about grades, consequences, or anything else. The emails are typically written in the form of a challenge, as if to say that their class is too difficult for *any* strategy or approach.

Now, there are, without a doubt, students with a proclivity to misbehave. There are students who are hurt and angry by sins done to them in the past and whose default setting is to rail against authority. But here's the thing, here's what I'd like to say to those teachers who are convinced that there is nothing they can do to stop certain students from being disrespectful: It takes two to tango.

Although it may not feel like you're contributing to the problem, if you show *any* outward sign of frustration or annoyance—even a sigh, a tightening of your jaw, or standoff-ishness—they assume that you're just like all the rest. They lump you together with all the other adults in their life who have scolded them, lectured them, battled them, and otherwise let them down. By proxy, you become the target of their anger. It may not be fair, or make much sense from your perspective, but it's reality.

Even pulling them aside and giving them a measured rebuke can push them to the point where, out of spite, they'll want nothing more than to prove to you that they really don't care. You see, they know that it's the one thing you can never control, the one thing that is guaranteed to hurt you and destroy the vision you have of yourself as a good and caring teacher. They have so much pride and youthful recklessness that they're willing to fail and endure any consequence just to not let you win or impose your will over them. And if you do lose your cool . . . if you do argue back or try to put them in their place, your relationship—and their behavior—will crater, until they won't even look at you anymore.

But the remarkable truth is, and what they keep hidden from anyone who doesn't understand where their behavior comes from, is that they do care. Sometimes more than any other student in your class. To tap into that treasure buried down deep inside, however, takes a complete release of animosity. It takes warm compassion in the face of disrespect. It takes standing alongside them rather than opposite them.

You have to prove to them through your words and actions that you're in their corner and that your modes of accountability aren't personal, but are for the benefit of every member of the class—including them.

It's your day-after-day kindness, gentleness, and good humor, when freely given no matter what's happening in their life or how they're behaving, that turns the tide. That wins them over. It's an unstoppable wave that crashes into that part of them that cares, that causes them to want to succeed, that instills in them a desire to please you and behave for you. Only when you remove yourself as an opponent, offering instead a leader they can trust, respect, and admire, will their behavior change, and change dramatically.

So, initially, how do you become that sort of person under the hot, harsh lights of disrespect, even hatred? Empathy. Empathy born of knowing what it feels like to be in their shoes, or imagining just how extraordinarily difficult it is, makes your refusal to *ever* create animosity and friction the easiest and most natural thing in the world. It's a strategy that works with the angriest, most wounded souls to ever enter a classroom.

And it works for every teacher, every time.

68

How to Handle Six Disrespectful Students in One Class

A READER EMAILED SCM WONDERING how to handle six students who were wreaking havoc in his classroom. Every day they were disruptive. They were talkative and silly. They called out during lessons and made inappropriate comments. They played off one another and held little regard for his expectations. Most distressing, when he'd confront them or attempt to hold them accountable, they would become disrespectful. They would argue and complain. They would lie and deny. They would talk back and then goof off when sent to time-out. The teacher was at the end of his rope and desperate for answers.

One or two disrespectful students are hard enough. How do you handle a half dozen who are determined to make your life miserable? Well, you don't, at least, not directly.

You see, one of the most common mistakes teachers make is trying to handle difficult students as distinct entities, separate from the class as a whole. Day after day, this teacher was pulling them aside for one-on-one talking-tos. He was lecturing them, counseling them, and giving them pep-talks. He set up behavior contracts, offered rewards in exchange for good behavior, and had consequences designed just for them. These individualized methods only make matters worse—because they *encourage* misbehavior. They cause resentment and antagonism. They wipe out intrinsic motivation and label students as "difficult," which becomes a self-fulfilling prophecy.

The truth is, when you have several or more students who consistently disrupt learning and behave disrespectfully, it's a sign you've lost control of your class—or never had it to begin with. It's a classroom management problem, not an individual student problem. The only way to fix it is to start over from the beginning. It's to establish sharply defined, non-negotiable boundaries of behavior *for all students* that are designed to protect your freedom to teach and your students' freedom to learn. Create a clear, no-nonsense classroom management plan that covers every possible misbehavior. Teach, model, and practice it so there are no misunderstandings or excuses not to follow it. Then defend it to the hilt. If you're in the middle of the school year, it may take several days to see results. You may even get considerable pushback, especially from the core of disrespectful students who have grown accustomed to having their way and dictating the environment of the class.

But if you fulfill your promise to protect the right of *every student* to learn and enjoy school, if you refrain from pulling students aside to scold, lecture, and bribe, and instead let your classroom management plan do your talking for you, then you'll begin to reel them in.

Your most well-behaved students will respond first. You'll notice them smiling more and making eye contact with you. They'll be more openly friendly and appreciative. They'll cheer you on from afar. Then a few more students will join in support. One by one, you'll begin picking them off and pulling them into your sphere of influence. Before long, just one of your most difficult students will turn things around. They'll abruptly start making the right choices. They'll become more respectful. They'll grow calmer, happier, and more responsive to you and your expectations. They'll like being part of the class. Then another difficult student will come aboard. Then another.

You'll now have more time and freedom to really enjoy your class and teach with greater passion. Your stress will fall away. You'll smile and laugh more often and begin building real influence and rapport with your students. You'll have *leverage*. Soon, the last few holdouts will take a look around and notice that no one is laughing at their jokes anymore. No one is amused by their antics.

They'll realize that following rules and participating as a valued member of the class is a better option than creating their own brand of fun or behaving rebelliously. They'll shrug their shoulders and join in too. After all, you've made their choice an easy one.

You've made the gap between the experience of being part of the class, and the experience of being held accountable, so wide that no student can resist. You've left the door to a safe, warm, and dry place wide open—where they're welcomed and accepted and can leave their baggage behind. Where they can be part of something special and bigger than themselves. Where their intrinsic motivational engines can finally begin to turn.

Thanks for reading *The Smart Classroom Management Way*! If you haven't done so already, please sign up for our newsletter at smartclassroommanagement.com

Made in United States
North Haven, CT
14 July 2022